COLONIALISM IN INDIA

Cover illustration: The Ear-Opener. Mr Gopal Krishna
Gokhakle, an Indian nationalist politician, attempting to
make it easire for John Bull to hear the demands being put
forward by the Indian National Congress. Cartoon from
Hindi Punch, December 1905.

COLONIALISM IN INDIA

A GCSE SOURCE BOOK FOR TEACHERS

S R Ashton

THE BRITISH LIBRARY

Published by
The British Library
Great Russell Street
London WC1B 3DG
and 27 South Main Street,
Wolfeboro, New Hampshire,
03894–2069 USA

British Library Cataloguing in Publication Data

Ashton, S. R. (Stephen R.)
   Colonialism in India: a GCSE source
   book for teachers.
   1. India, 1785–1947. Readings from
   contemporary sources
   I. Title
   954.03

ISBN 0–7123–0633–1

Designed by John Mitchell
Computer typeset by the author and Stephen Ashworth
with output generated on a Monotype Lasercomp
in Times New Roman at Oxford University Computing Service

Printed in Great Britain by
Antony Rowe Ltd
at Chippenham, Wiltshire

CONTENTS

NOTES FOR TEACHERS

The India Office Library and Records (IOLR) is the national centre for source material on the British involvement with India and with surrounding Asian countries for the period *c* 1600–1947. The Library and Record Office are two distinct but complementary collections, occupying the same building and sharing the same search and reading room facilities at 197 Blackfriars Road in London. Since April 1982 they have been a department of the Humanities and Social Sciences (formerly Reference) Division of the British Library. The IOLR works in close cooperation with Oriental Collections (formerly Oriental Manuscripts and Printed Books) which is also a department of the Humanities and Social Sciences Division. The department of Oriental Collections houses what is probably the most comprehensive collection of oriental material, in manuscript and printed form, in the world. The languages represented in the Collections are divided into five main geographical or cultural groups: Judaeo-Christian, Islamic, South Asian, South-East Asian and Far Eastern.

Together, the two departments – IOLR and Oriental Collections – provide an Education Service which aims to make their materials accessible to schools and colleges through publications, group visits, courses and seminars. The IOLR also offers individual guidance for teachers preparing course work, and students undertaking examination projects, on various aspects of South Asian History. Full details of the facilities offered by the Education Service at the IOLR, together with a brief description of the department's range of archival, library and visual materials, may be found in Steve Ashton and Penelope Tuson, *The India Office Library and Records: A Brief Guide for Teachers* (London: The British Library, 1985, reprinted 1987). Reference may also be made to S R Ashton, 'Archives and Education: The India Office Library and Records', in *Teaching History* (No 47, February 1987, pp 19–22).

This book has been prepared by the IOLRs Education Service in response to several enquiries from teachers requesting suitable primary source materials for the GCSE examination. The vast majority of the enquiries have been from teachers preparing candidates for the study on 'Colonialism' in the GCSE History Syllabus B devised by the Northern Examining Association (NEA). The objectives of this particular syllabus as defined by the board form the basis upon which the book has been written.

In the syllabus, a study of Colonialism forms one part (the other being a study of 'Human Rights') of the course work which is to be assessed internally by the candidate's teacher and then moderated by the boards of the NEA. The course work on Colonialism is based on a study of any one area of the world. The study is intended to illustrate various aspects of Colonialism ranging from the pre-colonial experience, the origins of colonialism and the colonial experience, the growth of nationalism and the achievement of independence, and, finally, the post-independence experience. India is by no means the only example of Colonialism but it is perhaps one of the more obvious. The enquiries received by the Education Service would seem to confirm that many centres have selected British colonialism in India as their example. This book does not cover the whole syllabus. It concentrates on the colonial experience in India and ends with the achievement of independence by India and Pakistan in August 1947.

The book has been prepared as a reference work for teachers. It assumes that the history of the Indian Subcontinent will be new to both teachers and their candidates. Each chapter therefore begins with an introductory narrative which is intended to serve as backround reading. The narratives are followed by a series of extracts drawn from a wide range of historical sources. These include the records of successive British administrations in India, private letters and diaries (both British and Indian), autobiographies and memoirs, photographs and prints, and newspaper cuttings and cartoons. Secondary sources have also been included. The two parts of each chapter are linked by a series of references which relate questions raised in the introductory narrative to the nature of the evidence as provided in the different extracts. The sources for the extracts are listed in the notes at the end of the book. Three devices have been employed to assist candidates with unfamiliar Indian names and terms and some of the more complex language in a number of extracts: first, square brackets within the extracts (a device most commonly used to explain Indian names and terms); secondly, explanatory notes either at the beginning or at the end of individual extracts; and, finally, a glossary which again appears at the end of the book.

The assessment objectives defined for the course work by the board are designed to test the candidate's ability upon the basis of the following criteria: first, the ability to collect and collate information on a particular historical problem and to deploy it in a clear and coherent form; secondly, the ability to interpret and evaluate a variety of historical sources; thirdly, the ability to reconstruct past events as seen from the perspective of people in the past; and finally, to make use of historical information in order to demonstrate an understanding of such concepts as cause and consequence, continuity and change and similarity and difference. The extracts included throughout the chapters in this book are designed to test the ability of candidates according to the first three criteria. For the fourth, the concepts of cause and consequence are examined in chapter 4 on the Rebellion of 1857 and chapter 7 on the Amritsar Massacre. The concepts of continuity and change are examined in chapter 3 on the Early Years of British Rule, chapter 5 on the Indian Economy and chapter 10 on the Transfer of Power. For an explanation of why Colonialism came to an end in India in 1947, chapters 5 and 10 should be read together. The concepts of similarity and difference are examined in chapter 8 on Gandhi and chapter 9 on Muslim separatism.

This book makes no attempt to set questions and exercises for the candidates or to suggest different teaching methods and approaches for the teacher. The Education Service at the IOLR draws a distinction between the role of a record office in this sort of exercise, and the role of a teacher. A record office can provide advice and guidance on the location of source material. It can also make this material accessible through publications of which this book is one example. But a record office cannot put itself in the position of a teacher in the classroom. The decision about the most suitable methods of presenting the materials provided by a record office must rest with the individual teacher, using his or her professional expertise and experience.

However, the distinction made between the role of a record office and that of a teacher does not rule out cooperation between the two. In recent years the Education Service has cooperated with a number of history teachers and history advisers in preparing publications on different aspects of Indian history. The details are listed in the bibiography at the end of this book. The Education Service would be willing to extend such cooperation by advising and supplying source material for a series of document or work packs on the subjects covered in this book or on any other subject for which there is a demand. The post-independence period in India and Pakistan would be an obvious example. Teachers, advisers or any other educational bodies interested in such work are invited to contact Dr Ashton at the India Office Library and Records, 197 Blackfriars Road, London SE1 8NG.

Steve Ashton
India Office Library and Records
July 1987

CHAPTER ONE

PRE-COLONIAL INDIA

The British period in India began in 1600 when the East India Company was established. It ended in 1947 when India and Pakistan became independent. The British connection with India represents but a fraction of the history of India. Indian history dates back over 4000 years. This chapter sketches a brief outline of this history and attempts to show some of the achievements of Indian civilisation before the arrival of the British at the beginning of the seventeenth century.

Ancient India

India represents one of the oldest civilisations in the world. One of the world's great river valley civilisations – the Indus Valley – flourished between 2500 and 1700 BC. Archaeologists excavated the Indus cities of Harappa and Mohenjo-daro in the 1920s. They discovered small stone seals which have picture images on them, of both humans and animals, and also a brief written script. To date, no one has been able to decipher the script. It is assumed that the seals were used by merchants for commercial or trading purposes. Indus seals have been discovered at the sites of the Mesopotamian civilisation in the Middle East which was older than that of the Indus but which flourished at the same time. The seals are an important piece of evidence to show that the two civilisations traded with each other.

Archaeologists have also attempted to explain how the Indus Valley civilisation came to an end. One argument suggests that flooding was the reason, another that the Indus cities were destroyed by Aryan invaders from Central Asia who began migrating into India in about 1500 BC. Whatever the reason, from the end of the Indus Valley civilisation, there followed a long, dark period in India's history, about which little is known. But from about 300 BC the picture becomes clearer. Evidence survives in the form of sculptures, written accounts by Indians themselves and also the accounts of early travellers who visited India. Alexander the Great of ancient Greece led an army into north-western India in about 327 BC. The Greeks made no lasting impression but some of those who accompanied Alexander's army recorded their impressions of what life in India was like (No 1). From around 320 BC a great Indian empire developed. It was known as the Mauryan empire. The most famous of the Mauryan kings was Asoka who reigned between 270 and 232 BC. Asoka made himself known by a series of edicts and inscriptions which appeared on rock pillars throughout his empire. One of the inscriptions tells of his conversion to Buddhism after he had defeated one of his enemies in a war in which thousands were killed. Asoka was sickened by the slaughter and this led him to become a Buddhist. Another great empire – that of the Guptas – flourished from the fourth to the sixth century AD. The Gupta period is often referred to as the Golden Age of ancient India. Art, literature and sculpture reached new levels of cultural achievement. Living standards were high, particularly for the upper classes.

As well as the Indus Valley civilisation and the great empires of the Mauryas and the Guptas, ancient India gave to the world two of its oldest religions – Hinduism and Buddhism – and one of its oldest languages – Sanskrit. It contributed much more besides, in ways which might come as a surprise to those who know little of India's history (Nos 2–5).

Muslim India

Throughout its history, India became accustomed to foreign invaders and settlers. Some, like the Greeks, did not remain long enough to make an impact. Others made a more lasting impression. It was a two-way process. The newcomers made new contributions to the development of Indian culture but they were also influenced by what they found in India when they arrived. Before the arrival of the Europeans in the seventeenth century, the most important newcomers were Muslims.

The Arabs were the first Muslims to arrive in India. They occupied the area of Sind in the eighth century. But the Muslims who made a more lasting impression came from Central Asia. Muslim invasions and migrations from this region became a recurring feature of Indian history from the eleventh century. They gave rise to the Mughal empire in India which was founded by the emperor Babur who ruled between 1526 and 1530. Mughal was the Persian word for Mongol. Babur was descended from Chingis Khan and Tamurlane, the Mongol warlords of Central Asia in the thirteenth and fourteenth centuries. At the beginning, the Mughal empire was but the latest in a line of Muslim empires which had ruled various parts of northern India since the eleventh century.

However, by the end of the seventeenth century, the Mughal empire had extended to virtually the whole of the Indian subcontinent (fig 1.1). The size, wealth and power of the empire dazzled a succession of travellers from Europe (Nos 6–9).

But there was more to the Mughals than extravagant displays of wealth and power. The emperor Akbar is generally regarded as the greatest of the Mughals. During Akbar's reign between 1556 and 1605, the Mughal empire set an example to Europe through its policies of political and religious toleration. Akbar was a soldier king. He fought wars against the Hindu warriors of Rajputana (now Rajasthan) who were known as Rajputs. But once he had defeated them in battle, Akbar extended the hand of friendship to the Rajputs. He made marriage alliances with them. Jehangir, Akbar's son and heir, was born of a Rajput princess. Akbar also appointed some of the Rajput princes as ministers in his government, as governors of his provinces and as military commanders in his army (Nos 10–11). There were, of course, sound political reasons why Akbar acted in this way. The Muslims were in a minority in India and cooperation with the Rajput princes was one of the ways in which Akbar was able to put his empire on a secure footing. But Akbar's tolerant policies extended to matters of religion (fig 1.2) and it was here that the contrast with Europe lay (Nos 12–13). In Europe at this time, kings and princes imposed their own religious beliefs on their subjects. They knew no other way of ensuring their loyalty. Heretics were burnt at the stake, Jewish communities were expelled from a number of countries and long, bloody wars were fought over religion.

Akbar's policies were continued during the reigns of Jehangir (1605–27) and Shah Jahan (1627–58) but were undone during the reign of Aurangzeb (1658–1707). Aurangzeb thought of himself as a model Muslim ruler and he was more strict on matters of religion. Under Akbar, Hindus had been treated as equals. Under Aurangzeb, they were merely tolerated. Aurangzeb spent most of the second half of his reign campaigning against two Hindu kingdoms in the far south of India. He also faced a rebellion by the Marathas in western India. The Marathas represented a new Hindu military force and they were skilled in the art of guerrilla warfare. Aurangzeb's wars were costly and they imposed a severe strain on the empire's finances. The seeds of Mughal decline had been sown. After Aurangzeb's death, the empire began to fragment. Men who had governed provinces of the empire in the name of the emperor broke away and declared their independence. They fought wars against their neighbours to carve out still more territory for themselves. The empire was also weakened by two lightning blows struck from outside. The Persians raided the Mughal capital of Delhi in 1738–9 and the Afghans did the same in 1756–7. A number of European trading companies had been established in India by this time. These companies were armed with soldiers of their own and they took sides in the wars being fought by rival Indian princes. The British, in the form of the East India Company, came out on top. They gradually emerged as the succesors to the Mughal empire. How and why this happened are questions which are examined in chapter 2.

India on the eve of Colonialism

Dating British colonialism in India is not as straightforward as it might appear. We have a definite date for the end of colonialism: August 1947 when India and Pakistan became independent. But when exactly did British colonialism in India begin? For the first 150 or so years of the British involvement with India – from 1600 to the middle of the eighteenth century – the British were certainly not rulers. They were small groups of traders, tucked away in small coastal settlements, with little power or influence. The rise of the British as a political and military power in India dates from the second half of the eighteenth century. It was a gradual process, which started in Bengal and then spread to other areas. In 1757, Robert Clive defeated the ruler of Bengal at the battle of Plassey. Nine years later, in 1765, the Mughal emperor granted the *diwani* of Bengal to the East India Company. The *diwani* put the Company in the position of tax gatherers and gave them financial control of Bengal. British colonialism in India dates from about this time.

The level of India's economic development on the eve of colonialism is a subject about which historians disagree. Some have suggested that India was a great manufacturing country and that it had reached a level of development which made an industrial revolution a possibility. They argue that colonialism prevented this from happening. Others have suggested that an industrial revolution was unlikely because the Indian economy was backward in several ways. The views of historians, as well as some contemporary European accounts of different trades and farming methods in India before the age of colonialism, are reproduced in Nos 14–19.

THE GREEKS IN ANCIENT INDIA

1. Nearchus, Alexander the Great's admiral, describing the clothes worn by the people of India in about 327 BC

The dress worn by the Indians is made of cotton produced on trees. But this cotton is either of a brighter white colour than any found anywhere else, or the darkness of the Indian complexion makes their apparel [clothing] look so much whiter. They wear an undergarment of cotton which reaches below the knee halfway down to the ankles and an upper garment which they throw partly over their shoulders and partly twist in folds

4

Map labels: Kabul, Peshawar, Kandahar (Persia), Independent Pathan Tribes, R. Jhelum, R. Chenab, R. Ravi, Lahore, R. Beas, Multan, R. Sutlej, R. Indus, Panipat, Delhi, JATS, RAJPUTS, Agra, R. Jumna, R. Chambal, Gogra, R. Gogra, Gumti, Allahabad, Benares, Patna, Chanderingore (French), Calcutta (British), Serampore (Danish), R. Nerbudda, Tributary Chiefs of Gondwana, Mahanadi, R. Tapti, Surat, Daman (Portuguese), Bassein (Portuguese), Diu Is. (Portuguese), Bombay (British), MARATHAS, R. Godavari, R. Kistna, Goa (Portuguese), R. Tungabhadra, Pulicat (Dutch), Madras (British), Sadras (Dutch), Pondicherry (French), R. Cauvery, Calicut, Tranquebar (Danish), Negapatam (Dutch), Cochin (Dutch), POLYGARS

THE
MUGHAL EMPIRE
AT THE END OF
THE
SEVENTEENTH CENTURY

Approximate Boundaries ▬ ▬ ▬ ▬ ▬
European Settlements Thus — Madras (British)
In Revolt RAJPUTS

1.1 The Mughal Empire at the end of the 17th century.

round their head. The Indians also wear earrings of ivory, but only the very wealthy do this. They use parasols as a screen from the heat. They wear shoes made of white leather and these are elaborately trimmed, while the soles are ... made of great thickness, to make the wearer seem much taller.

MATHEMATICS IN ANCIENT INDIA

2. From Jawaharlal Nehru, 'The Discovery of India'. Nehru was India's first Prime Minister when the British left and India became independent in 1947

Europe got its early arithmetic and algebra from the Arabs – hence the 'Arabic numerals' – but the Arabs themselves had previously taken them from India. The astonishing progress that the Indians had made in mathematics is now well known and it is recognised that the foundations of modern arithmetic and algebra were laid long ago in India. The clumsy method of using a counting frame and the use of Roman and such like numerals had long retarded [held back] progress when the ten Indian numerals, including the zero sign, liberated the human mind from these restrictions ... These number symbols were unique and entirely different from all other symbols that had been in use in other countries. They are common enough today and we take them for granted, yet they contained the germs [origins] of revolutionary progress in them. It took many centuries for them to travel from India, via Baghdad, to the western world.

3. From A L Basham, 'The Wonder that was India'

The debt of the Western world to India in this respect cannot be overestimated. Most of the great discoveries of which Europe is proud would have been impossible without a developed system of mathematics, and this in turn would have been impossible if Europe had been shackled [held back] by the unwieldy [clumsy] system of Roman numerals. The unknown man who devised the new system was from the world's point of view, after the Buddha, the most important son of India. His achievement, though easily taken for granted ... deserves much more honour than [it] has so far received.

ANCIENT INDIAN MEDICINE

4. From A L Basham, 'The Wonder that was India'. By 'judicial mutilation', Basham means a punishment, like the cutting off of a hand, for a crime, such as theft

[P]lastic surgery was developed far beyond anything known elsewhere at this time.

1.2   Jesuit priests (in the foreground) discussing matters of religion at the Mughal court, by a Mughal artist, c. 1608.

Ancient Indian surgeons were expert at the repair of noses, ears and lips, lost or injured in battle or by judicial mutilation. In this respect Indian surgery remained ahead of Europe until the 18th century, when the surgeons of the East India Company were not ashamed to learn the art of rhinoplasty [plastic surgery of the nose] from the Indians.

5. *T A Wise, a surgeon employed by the East India Company in India, writing in 1845*

[I]t appears that at a very early age the Hindus had made much greater advances in civilization and the arts and sciences than any other ancient people; and while the nations of the west have been slowly advancing in civilization during the last two thousand years, the Hindus, by the depressing influence of foreign subjugation [foreign rule], are at present in a lower social condition than they appear to have been in, three centuries before the Christian era. It was most probably at this early period that they studied the healing art with such success as to enable them to produce systematic works on medicine ... the ancient system of Hindu medicine was so complete in all its parts, and so permanent in its influence ... that several centuries were required to form it.

THE MUGHAL EMPIRE

6. *Ralph Fitch, an Elizabethan traveller, was the first Englishman on record to visit India. He arrived in 1583 when the emperor Akbar was on the throne. He wrote the following account of the cities of Agra and Fatepore (today, Fatehpur Sikri). By 'Moors', Fitch means Muslims; by 'Gentiles', he means Hindus.*

Agra is a very great city and populous, built with stone, having fair and large streets, with a fair river running by it, which falls into the Gulf of Bengal. It has a fair castle and a strong [keep], with a very fair ditch [moat]. Here be many Moors and Gentiles. The King is called Zelabdim Echebar [Jalaluddin Akbar]; the people for the most part call him the Great Moghul. From thence we went to Fatepore, which is the place where the King keeps his court. The town is bigger than Agra, but the houses and streets be not so fair. Here dwell many people, both Moors and Gentiles. The King has in Agra and Fatepore (as they do credibly report) 1000 elephants, thirty thousand horses, 1400 tame deer, 800 concubines [mistresses]: such store of ounces [cheetahs], tigers, buffaloes, cocks and hawks, that is very strange to see. He keeps a great court which they call Dericcan [Persian for palace]. Agra and Fatepore are two very great cities, either of them much greater than London and very populous. Between Agra and Fatepore are 12 miles, and all the way is full of victuals [food supplies] and other things, as full as though a man were still in a town, and so many people as if a man were in a market. They have many fine carts, and many of them carved and gilded with gold, with two wheels, which be drawn with two little bulls about the size of our great dogs in England, and they will run with any horse, and carry two or three men in one of these carts; they are covered with silk or very fine cloth, and be used here as coaches are in England. Here is great resort [meeting place] of merchants from Persia and beyond India, and very much merchandise of silk and cloth, and of precious stones, both rubies, diamonds and pearls.

7. *Sir Thomas Roe describing the size of the Mughal empire during the reign of the emperor Jehangir (1605–27). Roe was the Ambassador of King James I at the court of Jehangir between 1615 and 1619*

His territory is far greater than the Persians, and almost as equal, if not as great, as the Turks. His means of money, by revenue [taxation], the custom of [giving] Presents, and inheriting all mens' goods, superior to both. His Country lies West to Sind, and so stretches to Candahar [in Persia], and to the Mountains of Taurus North; to the East as far as the utmost parts of Bengal, and the borders of the Ganges; and South to the Deccan. It is two thousand square miles at the least, but has many petty [small] kings within, that are Tributaries.

8. *Edward Terry, a priest, who visited India between 1616 and 1619, describing Jehangir's empire*

The Great Moghul, considering his territories, his wealth, and his rich commodities, is the greatest known King of the east, if not of the world … This wide monarchy is very rich and fertile; so much abounding in all necessaries for the use of man as that it is able to subsist [exist] and flourish of itself, without the least help of any neighbour …

9. *Sir Thomas Roe's description of the emperor Jehangir*

The King descended the stairs with such an acclamation [greeting] of 'health to the King' as would have out-cried canons. At the stair's foot, where I met him, and shuffled to be next [to be introduced], one brought a mighty carp [fish]; another a dish of white stuff like starch, into which he put his finger, and touched the fish and so rubbed it on his forehead, a ceremony used presaging [a sign of] good fortune. Then another came and buckled on his sword and buckler, set all over with diamonds and rubies, the belts of gold suitable. Another hung his quiver with 30 arrows and his bow in a case, the same that was presented by the Persian ambassador. On his head he wore a rich turban with a plume of heron tops, not many but long; on one side a ruby unset, as big as a walnut; on the other side a diamond as great; in the middle an emerald like a heart, much bigger. His sash was wreathed about with a chain of great pearl, rubies, and diamonds drilled. About his neck he carried a chain of most excellent pearl, three double (so great I never saw): at his elbows, armlets set with diamonds; and on his wrists three rows of several sorts. His hands bare, but on almost every finger a ring; his gloves, which were English, stuck under his girdle.

THE EMPEROR AKBAR

10. *Niccolao Manucci, an Italian traveller in India in the seventeenth century, recalling Akbar's relations with the Hindu Princes*

If any of the Mughal Kings inherited the valour and judgment of Timur [Tamurlane] ... it was ... Akbar ... This king ... allied himself to several Rajput princes, thus bringing them over to his side. With their aid he conquered the greater part of Hindustan, routing the remaining Afghans in different battles and bringing them into subjection to his orders. So great was the dread in which Akbar was held by the Hindu princes that they came voluntarily giving him their daughters. He received them all with open arms, but he forced them to fight against the other Hindu princes, aiding them with his own army.

11. *The promotion of Raja Todar Mal, a Hindu prince, as described by Abul Fazl, one of Akbar's favourites, who wrote two histories of Akbar's reign. The diwan was the emperor's revenue minister, with responsibility for collecting taxes*

Raja Todar Mal now arrived at Court, bringing with him fifty-four elephants, which had been taken [during a campaign] in Bengal. These he presented, and he made a report upon the state of the country. He received many marks of favour, and was promoted to the dignity of *diwan*, and to the charge of the revenue and civil affairs of the Empire.

12. *The abolition of religious taxes, described by Abul Fazl*

It was an old standing custom for the [Muslim] rulers of Hindustan to exact contributions, according to their respective means [their ability to pay] from the pilgrims who visited the [Hindu] holy shrines. This tax was called *karmi*. His Majesty's judgment and equity [sense of justice] condemned this exaction ... An order was accordingly issued abolishing it throughout his dominions ... He was pleased to say that although this was a tax on the vain and superstitions of the multitude, and the devotees [worshippers] did not pay it except when they travelled ... still the course they adopted was their mode [method] of worshipping the Almighty, and the throwing of a stumbling-block and obstacle in their way could never be acceptable in the sight of God ...

One of the munificent [most generous] acts of the Emperor at the beginning of this the ninth year of his reign was the remission [abolition] of the *jizya* [a tax upon non-Muslims], which, in a country so extensive as Hindustan, amounted to an immense sum.

13. *Akbar's interest in other religions, as described by Father Monserrate, a Portugese Jesuit who spent two years at Akbar's court between 1580 and 1582. The Jesuits were members of a Roman Catholic order who acted as missionaries for the Roman Catholic church. Akbar held regular meetings to discuss religion with men of different faiths. The Jesuits took this as a sign that they might convert him to Christianity. They were mistaken*

The King was always pondering in his mind which nation has retained the true religion of God; and to this question he constantly gave the most earnest thought. He devised the following ingenious method of settling the problem. On a certain night he ordered all the nobles, the religious leaders both of Hindus and Musalmans, and the Christian priests to be summoned to the inner palace. He placed the nobles in line according to their rank, bade all the wise men and doctors of religion take their places before him, and then asked them questions on various points ...

At the conclusion of the discussion the King briefly addressed all who had been present. He said: 'I perceive [see] that there are varying customs and beliefs of varying religious paths. For the teachings of the Hindus, the Musalmans, the Jazdini [Parsis], the Jews and the Christians are all different. But the followers of each religion regard the institutions of their own religion as better than those of any other. Not only so, but they strive to convert the rest to their own way of belief. If these refuse to be converted, they not only despise them, but also regard them for this very reason as their enemies. And this causes me to feel many serious doubts and scruples [uncertainty]. Wherefore I desire that on appointed days the books of all the religious laws be brought forward, and that the doctors meet together and hold discussions, so that I might hear them, and that each one may determine which is the truest and mightiest religion ...'

On the next day he again summoned several doctors belonging to other sects to be summoned together with the priests. When they had arrived he said to the priests: 'I desire that we should now begin to carry out my proposal of yesterday ... God knows that I am sincere in my will and intentions regarding this determination which I have made.' At the moment when he said this his two eldest sons were sitting by his side and several chieftans and petty kings were standing around him. The priests ... at once began the proposed course of lectures and discussions with an exposition [explanation] of the Gospel. However the others gradually ceased coming to the appointed place, and the Christians alone gladly obeyed the King's desire ... However the priests began to suspect that he was intending to found a new religion with matter taken from all the existing systems; and hence they also gradually withdrew themselves from the meetings.

THE INDIAN ECONOMY ON THE EVE OF COLONIALISM

14. Morris D Morris, an American historian. By 'technology', Morris means machinery using mechanical or water power. By 'productivity' he means output or the amount of goods produced. 'Manual dexterity' means skilled at working with the hands

There is a widespread notion [belief] that India was a great preindustrial manufacturing nation. It is much more likely that in the eighteenth century India had achieved a technology that was at about the productive levels of late medieval Europe. If one looks at European technical development between 1400 and 1700 and compares these with what India possessed in the eighteenth century, one can see the truth of this. While India produced fine textiles and a few examples of remarkable craftmanship, we must not mistake manual dexterity for productivity nor assume that dexterity implied the presence of sophisticated tools and manufacturing techniques. In fact the reverse is true. Finally, geography and climate made for an inefficient system of waterways and roads, useful only during very limited periods of the year.

15. T Raychaudhuri, an Indian historian, commenting on Morris's views. By 'scant justice', Raychaudhuri means not recognising the importance of

[Morris's] view does scant justice to the fact that India was the major supplier of textiles – not just of fine cloths, but everyday wear for the masses – to the whole of South East Asia, Iran, the Arab countries and East Africa ... European ... trade opened up fresh markets for the same commodity in Europe, West Africa, the New World [North America], the Philippines and Japan.

16. T Raychaudhuri, commenting on India's limitations. By 'manufactures', Raychaud-huri means India's textile industry which was still based on hand-worked looms. By 'inanimate', he means that the only form of power used by Indians was that based on animals (horses, oxen, elephants etc). By 'spontaneous movement' he means happening on its own without outside help

On the debit [minus] side, India failed to produce proper cast-iron, manufacture the glassware which fascinated her royalty and aristocracy, use her coal despite the availability of surface deposits ... In sharp contrast to China, mechanical clocks from Europe – much admired toys in the Mughal courts – were never imitated or taken apart out of curiosity. Nautical instruments like the compass and the telescope were known but never used ...

A ... factor inhibiting [preventing] technological change was the tradition of minutely [very small] specialized hereditary skills built into the caste system ...

India had not witnessed any agricultural revolution. Her technology – in agriculture and manufactures – had by and large been stagnant [had not progressed] for centuries. For a country so advanced in civilization, the technology was also rather primitive. The use of inanimate power in any form was virtually unknown ... in the long run the manual skill of the Indian artisan [labourer] was no substitute for technological progress ... No ... scientific revolution formed part of the eighteenth century Indian's historical experience ... Spontaneous movement towards industrialisation is unlikely in such a situation.

17. Francis Pelseart, a Dutch merchant in India between 1620 and 1627, commenting on the various craft trades of Agra. By painters he means painters of cloth who produced chintzes (see the introduction to chapter 2)

Goldsmiths, painters, embroiderers, carpet-makers, cotton or silk-weavers, blacksmiths, coppersmiths, tailors, masons, builders, stone-cutters, a hundred crafts in all, for a job which one man would do in Holland here passes through four men's hands before it is finished.

18. John Ovington, an East India Company chaplain in India between 1690 and 1693, explaining why printing presses had not been adopted in India

Neither have they [the Indians] endeavoured to transcribe [copy] our Art of Printing; that would diminish the Repute [status] and Livelihood of their Scribes [writers or clerks], who maintain numerous families by the Pen. But they can imitate a little the English manner of binding books.

19. Francis Buchanan, an East India Company medical officer in India between 1794 and 1806, describing farming methods

Immediately after the ... crop has been reaped, the ploughings commence; and are carried on exactly as before ... only in place of one man's standing on the plank drawn by oxen, the ground being now harder, three or four men must stand on this instrument ... In India it is seldom that an attempt is made to accomplish anything by machinery, that can be performed by hand.

CHAPTER TWO

THE ORIGINS OF COLONIALISM

Trade with India: The East India Company

An English East India Company was established by royal charter on the last day of 1600. The merchants who put up money for the Company wanted a share of the spice trade with the East Indies, present-day Indonesia. They did not succeed because of competition from a more powerful Dutch trading company. Instead, the English East India Company turned its attention towards India.

India also had spices but textiles were the main trading attraction. Indian *chintzes* were in great demand in Europe. A *chintz* was a hand-painted cotton fabric which did not run when washed. *Chintzes* were of a superior quality to the dyed fabrics produced at this time in Europe. They were admired by the English because of their clear colours and because they could withstand repeated washing. Indian patterns were not always to the liking of the Europeans. Samples of Western patterns were therefore sent out to India to be copied by Indian artists. The finished products, a mixture of Indian and European design, were used as bedspreads, wall-hangings and dress materials. In addition, India had indigo, a blue dye; saltpetre, which was used in the manufacture of gunpowder; rice and sugar cane. It also had opium which was exported, illegally, to China in return for tea. Huge quantities of tea were sent back to England in the eighteenth century and tea-drinking became part of the British way of life.

The East India Company sent envoys to the court of the Mughal emperors to request trading rights. The Company wanted permission to establish factories. A factory was a trading post where goods were stored before being shipped home. Permission was granted and, during the seventeenth century, a handful of British settlements grew up. They were located on the Indian coasts – on the west coast at Surat and Bombay, on the east coast at Fort St George in Madras, and further north at Fort William (Calcutta) in Bengal.

The Rise of the East India Company as a Political Power

At the beginning of the eighteenth century the East India Company was still confined to these coastal settlements. The inhabitants who lived and worked in these settlements numbered scarcely more than a few hundred. Aurangzeb, the Mughal emperor who ruled between 1658 and 1707, was still on the throne. The British were not the only European power with trading interests in India. The French (the main rivals to the British), Danes, Dutch and Portugese also occupied small coastal settlements. However, by the beginning of the nineteenth century the position had changed dramatically. The Mughal empire had declined and the French had been defeated. The East India Company, while not in possession of the entire subcontinent, had emerged as the strongest political power in India (fig 2.1). The reasons for this change represent the origins of colonialism in India.

The Origins of Colonialism – How and Why?

The Court of Directors – the men who managed the affairs of the East India Company in London – always denied that political power in India was their objective (No 1). In explaining why this eventually happened, a distinction must be drawn between the reasons which enabled the British to obtain political power (Nos 2–3) and the reasons why they made the attempt (Nos 4–5). The two are not necessarily the same thing. The problem of communication, both within India and between Britain and India, was an important part of the process (No 6).

In India, the men who worked for the East India Company were known as the Company's servants. The majority worked as traders. They bought and sold goods and handled the Company's accounts. The others were soldiers, sailors, doctors and priests. It was difficult for the Court of Directors in London to exercise real control over its servants in India. At times these servants behaved as if they were a law unto themselves. Young men went out to India expecting to make a fortune (No 7). Fortunes were indeed made, often by corrupt and dishonest means (No 8). As individuals became richer, the East India Company itself began to run into debt. The wars being fought in the Company's name were very costly. It was also expensive to run the new territories which came under Company control. In Britain, the affairs of the Company began to attract criticism and a number of enquiries were set up. The most famous was the impeachment of Warren Hastings, the first Governor-General of India (1774–85). Hastings was made the scapegoat for everything that was wrong. At the end of the eighteenth century the Company was brought under the control of Parliament in London. Increasingly, the men who worked for the Company ceased to be traders. Instead they became civil servants. It was their job to collect taxes and to adminster justice in the Company's territories. In 1834 the Company's trading functions in India were abolished. Trade with India was left in private hands. Until 1858, the Company was in effect the British Government in India.

THE OBJECTIVES OF THE EAST INDIA COMPANY

1. *Despatch from the Court of Directors in London to the Governor-General and his Council in Bengal, 21 July 1786*

The one universal principle never to be departed from, either in the present condition of the native powers or in any future relations amongst them, is that we are completely satisfied with the possessions we already have and will engage in no war for the purpose of further acquisitions ... The next leading principle is to keep a constant watch upon the conduct of all European rivals, particularly the French. As they cannot possibly interfere in the disputes of any of the native princes without harming our interests, it seems to follow as a just conclusion that if any of the native princes accepts European aid, we shall feel obliged to throw the aid of our force into the opposite scale. It ought to be emphasised in every transaction with them that the acceptance of any such aid can only be with the risk of having our whole force employed to crush the effects of it ... It should be generally known and understood that peace is our primary object. We wish to pursue the interchanges of trade beneficial to them and to us and to render [make] those parts of India which are within our immediate administration completely happy under the protection of British power. We shall refrain from all interference in the disputes which may arise amongst the native princes and we shall not take advantage of their jealousies in order to extend British power at the expense of any one of them ... The security of our possessions must be our only object, and not ideas of splendour, aggrandisement [increase in power] or ambition.

THE GROWTH OF BRITISH POWER IN INDIA: THE REASONS WHICH MADE IT POSSIBLE

2. *The views of P J Marshall, a British historian*

The question of why British territorial expansion in eighteenth century India became possible can hardly be answered except in terms of Anglo–French rivalry and Mughal decline. Without the threat posed by the French, the British troops and ships which

INDIA 1765 Territorial gains made at the time of Clive

INDIA 1805 Territorial gains made at the time of Wellesley

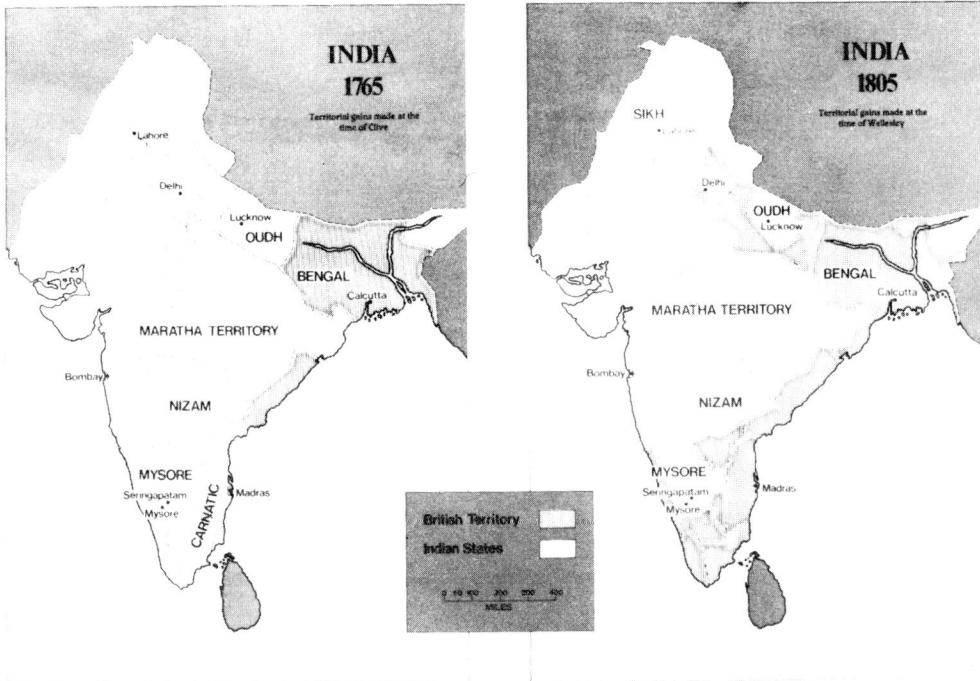

2.1 *The growth of British territorial power in India: 1765, 1805 and 1857.*

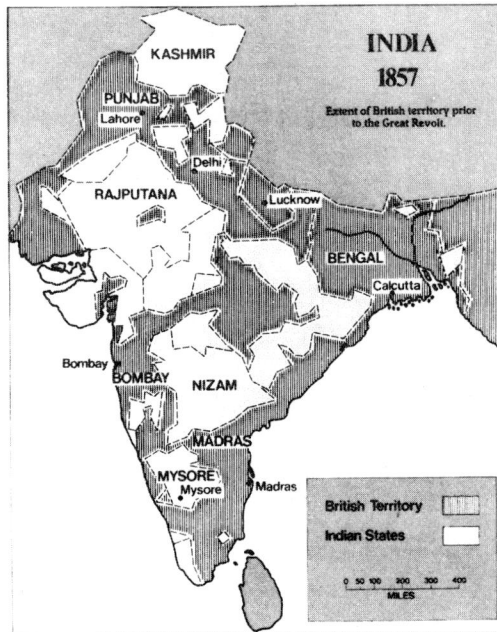

INDIA 1857 Extent of British territory prior to the Great Revolt.

played so important a role would never have been despatched to India, nor would the authorities at home have sanctioned [approved] the expense of maintaining the new armies in India. Spending on such a scale would not have been tolerated merely to win concessions for British trade.

3. *The views of Jawaharlal Nehru*

Looking back over this period, it almost seems that the British succeeded in dominating India by a succession of fortuitous [fortunate] circumstances and lucky flukes. With remarkably little effort, considering the glittering prize, they won a great empire and enormous wealth, which helped to make them the leading power in the world. It seems easy for a slight turn of events to have taken place which would have dashed their hopes and ended their ambitions. They were defeated on many occasions – by Haider Ali and Tipu [Hindu rulers of the kingdom of Mysore in the south], by the Marathas [a warlike Hindu race from central and south-western India], by the Sikhs [of the Punjab] and by the Gurkhas [of Nepal]. A little less of good fortune and they might have lost their foothold in India, or at the most held on to certain coastal settlements only.

And yet a closer scrutiny reveals a certain inevitability in what happened. Good fortune there certainly was, but there must be an ability to profit by good fortune. India was then in a fluid and disorganised state, following the break-up of the Mughal Empire: for centuries it had not been so weak and helpless. Organised power having broken down, the field was left open to adventurers and new claimants for dominion. Among these adventurers and claimants, the British, and the British alone, possessed many of the qualities necessary for success ...

The East India Company ... extended the territory under its control, chiefly by taking sides in local disputes, helping one rival against another. The Company's troops were better trained and were an asset to any side, and the Company extracted heavy payment for the help. So the Company's power grew and its military establishment increased.

Anti-foreign sentiment there undoubtedly was, and this grew in later years; but it was far removed from any general or widespread national feeling. The background was feudal and loyalty went to the local chief. Widespread distress ... compelled people to join any military leader who offered regular pay or opportunities of loot. The East India Company's armies largely consisted of Indian *sepoys* [soldiers]. Only the Marathas had some national sentiment, something much more than loyalty to a leader, behind them, but even this was narrow and limited. They managed to irriate the brave Rajputs [Hindu warriors] by their treatment of them. Instead of gaining them as allies, they had to deal with them as opponents or as grumbling and dissatisfied fuedatories [subordinates]. Among the Maratha chiefs themselves there was bitter rivalry, and occasionally civil war, in spite of a vague alliance under the Peshwa's [the most senior

Maratha chief] leadership. At critical moments they failed to support each other, and were separately defeated.

THE GROWTH OF BRITISH POWER IN INDIA: THE REASONS WHY THEY MADE THE ATTEMPT

4. Robert Clive to William Pitt the Elder, the leader of a wartime coalition government in Britain, 7 January 1759

I flatter myself I have made it pretty clear to you that there will be little or no difficulty in obtaining the absolute possession of these rich kingdoms: and this with the Mughal's [the Emperor's] own consent, on condition of paying him less than a fifth of the revenues thereof. Now I leave you to judge whether an income of upwards of two millions sterling, with the possession of three provinces [Bengal, Bombay and Madras] abounding in the most valuable productions of nature and of art, be an object deserving the public attention; and whether it be worth the nation's while to take the proper measures to secure such an acquisition ; an acquisition which ... would prove a source of immense wealth to the kingdom, and might in time be appropriated [taken over] in part as a fund towards diminishing the heavy load of debt under which we at present labour. Add to these advantages the influence we shall thereby acquire over the several European nations engaged in the commerce here, which these could no longer carry on but through our indulgence [permission], and under such limitations as we should think fit to prescribe [lay down]. It is well worth consideration that this project may be brought about without draining the mother country [Britain], as has been too much the case with our possessions in America. A small force from home will be sufficient as we always make sure of any number we please of black troops, who, being both much better paid and treated by us than by the country [Indian] powers, will very readily enter our service.

5. The views of Percival Spear, a British historian

If there were good reasons why the British should be successful in their contest for the control of India we still have to consider why they made the attempt. The essential answer is commerce and vested interests ... If there had been no money in it, they would certainly have withdrawn. The Company's trade in India was no longer profitable, for its profits, instead of being augmented [increased] by the revenues of Bengal, were in fact absorbed by the costs of administration. Its profits came from China, where the tea trade increased rapidly ... While China provided tea for the Company it was willing to take opium from India. This trade, carried on indirectly in China, for it was repeatedly banned by the Chinese government, eventually more than paid for the Company's tea investment, and was responsible for its continued commercial prosperity. Here was something which could not be given up, something which was made more profitable by political control ...

To this motive of preserving existing trade must be added the hope of more to come. The private merchants of London looked longingly at the size of India ... and its population and were convinced that a great market lay waiting to be tapped ...

A third influence was that of vested interests ... Here was the powerful and independent shipping interest, upon whom the whole British position in India depended. Then there was the supply of stores for the administration, civil and military, which, owing to the absence of European equipment in India at that time, was on a very extensive scale. The cotton interest in England hoped for a larger market for its manufactured goods. And then there was the human vested interest of Indian service. Formerly men went to India to seek a fortune but more often found a grave. By 1800 increasing numbers sought a career in the Company's civil and military services.

THE PROBLEM OF COMMUNICATION

6. *The views of Judith M Brown, a British historian*

Certain themes recur over the centuries, whether the all-India rulers were Mogul, British or independent India's politicians. The subcontinent's sheer size and diversity mean that it will always be difficult to administer from an all-India centre ... Particularly was this true before swift communications between government and its servants, by metalled road, railway, telegraph, telephone, and air travel. The old saying, 'Delhi is far off', referred to the Mogul government and its capital. It can still apply.

Two aspects of the British presence were always important ... Given the distance from England, and the voyage of up to three months which separated the Company's servants in India from Westminster and Leadenhall Street [the headquarters of the Company in the City of London], it was normally the men on the spot who made the key political and military decisions. Men such as Clive, Warren Hastings or Lord Wellesley had far more opportunity for initiative and manoeuvre than their successors who could not ignore the fast mail and telegraph. However, they in turn depended on information received from lowlier Company servants, sometimes far from Calcutta, who had substantial interests at stake in India in their private capacities. Such private interests were the other aspect of the British presence, a continuing part of the context and often a marked influence on the process of expansion.

THE COMPANY'S SERVANTS

7. *Stair Dalrymple, a seventeen-year-old Scotsman, to his brother, Sir Hugh Dalrymple, 1 November 1752*

This day, after very long suspense, I am appointed by the Directors of the United East India Company as a Writer [clerk] in their settlements in that place [India] ... I look upon myself now as a man of Business. I don't think a voyage to the East Indies is like the one I made to Norway for five or so weeks. I expect it to be a Duration of fifteen or twenty years at least. In that time I may be made Governour. If not that, I may make a Fortune which will make me live like a Gentleman ... We are obliged to serve the Company for the space of five years, for little or nothing recompense [payment or salary]. But that don't signifie much for we have the Liberty to Trade as much as we please and at the end of five years we may be great men by good Interest.

8. *A parliamentary enquiry into the affairs of the East India Company, 18 December 1772. Giving evidence, Samuel Wilks, the Company's Examiner of Indian Correspondence*

Mr Impey Does not Mr Wilks know ... that a tax has been laid upon the natives of India, which tax would bring in considerable sums to the Company; and likewise whether these sums have been accounted for to the Company?

Mr Wilks I find, in perusing the Company's papers, that there has been a tax arbitarily imposed upon the natives ... which tax it was said would bring in one million [rupees] per annum to the Company, and commenced from April 1765, although the Company was kept in ignorance of it until five years afterwards.

Mr Sykes Does Mr Wilks know how this money arising from the [tax] was applied and whether it was applied to the use of individuals, or that of the Company?

Mr Wilks Governor Sykes received annually 24,000 rupees for his table [his food and drink], 18,000 for his dress, and for his *moonshee* [Persian Secretary] 18,000 more, which makes in the whole 60,000 rupees annually paid him.

NOTE: A rupee was worth approximately 2 shillings [10 pence] so Governor Sykes received about £6000 in all for his personal expenses from this tax.

CHAPTER THREE

THE EARLY YEARS OF BRITISH RULE

An 'Age of Reform'?

Older historical accounts often refer to the first half of the nineteenth century in India as an 'Age of Reform'. These were said to be the years when India experienced, for the first time, the direct impact of Western influences and Western ideas. Particular significance is attached to the reforms introduced when Lord Bentinck was Governor-General of India between 1828 and 1835. But how great was the impact of British rule and is it accurate to speak of an 'Age of Reform'?

Two major questions faced the British during the first half of the nineteenth century. Large areas of India, but never the whole, were now under British control. How should these territories be governed and for what purpose? In Britain, these two questions produced two very different answers. Opinion was divided between the conservatives and the reformers.

Contrasting views of India

The conservatives were often men who had served in India. Their experience taught them that the British should be cautious. They argued that the East India Company should concentrate on maintaining peace and security in its own territories. They also argued that the Company should not interfere too directly in the lives of its Indian subjects. In particular, they warned about the dangers of missionary activity (Nos 1–2).

In contrast, the reformers wanted to go much further. They represented a number of influences. Some were Utilitarians, men who were influenced by the teachings of Jeremy Bentham (1748–1832). Bentham was an important political philosopher in Britain. He judged laws and government institutions soley in terms of how useful they were.

Utilitarian comes from the word to utilise or to use. By useful, Bentham meant that government should be organised and laws introduced in order to achieve 'the greatest happiness of the greatest number'. Other reformers were Evangelicals. The Evangelicals were strict Protestants. They held strong views about moral standards and about the observance of Sunday as the 'Lord's Day'. They believed in the death and resurrection of Jesus Christ as the only means of achieving personal salvation. The Evangelicals had two main aims: to abolish the slave trade and to open up India to missionary activity. The final group of reformers were Free Traders who wanted to open up India to British trade and commerce. Collectively, the reformers believed that Western beliefs and ideas were superior to those of the East. They regarded India as a backward country. Indian society was said to be incapable of improvement. The reformers wanted to reform India along Western lines: the Utilitarians, through efficient government (No 3); the Evangelicals through the Bible and missionaries (No 4); and the Free Traders through railways and roads which would enable still more trade to develop (No 5).

The Reforms

Gradually, the ideas of the reformers carried more weight than those of the conservatives. Western influences were introduced in a number of ways. Indian courts began to adopt British legal procedures. British legal experts began compiling a standard Indian Penal Code of criminal law. Pressure from the Evangelicals led in 1813 to the lifting of the ban on missionary work in India (fig 3.1). Campaigns were waged against a number of Hindu rituals. *Sati*, the burning of widows on the funeral pyres of their husbands, was outlawed in 1829 (No 6). Dependent on money from the land as their principal source of income, the British set up enquiries to determine who owned the land, who should pay rent and how much they should pay. The most important reform, certainly in the long-term, was the introduction of Western education through the English language. The British debate about the future of education in India produced two main groups or schools of thought. The first were the Orientalists who tended to be more conservative. They wanted a system of education based on Sanskrit and Arabic, the traditional languages of Indian learning. The second group were the Anglicists who saw themselves as reformers. They wanted a system of education based on Western literature and science. In 1835, the views of Thomas Babington Macaulay, the Law Member of the Governor-General's Council and the Chairman of the Committee of Public Instruction in Bengal, decided the issue in favour of the Anglicists (No 7). The reformers pinned large hopes on the development of Western education in India (Nos 8–9).

The 'Age of Reform' petered out in the 1840s. The British were involved in a series of wars in India. They were defeated in Afghanistan (1839–42) but conquered Sind (1843) and the Punjab (1845–49). Elsewhere, the British annexed a number of Indian princely kingdoms. These kingdoms were thought to be backward and the British believed that their subjects would be much better off under British rule. The 'doctrine of lapse' was often used as an excuse for the annexations. If a Hindu prince did not have a natural heir to his throne, the British did not allow him to adopt a successor. Instead, when the prince died, his kingdom was said to have 'lapsed' to British rule.

The limited impact of the Reforms

But how great was the impact of Western reforms upon Indian society? Intellectuals in London might debate what the British should do thousands of miles away in India but it was by no means easy to put their ideas into practice. On the one hand, the British did not have the money. The East India Company spent most of its money on administration and the army. There was little money left to introduce ambitious schemes of social and economic reform. On the other hand, the British did not have the manpower. Even at the height of British rule at the beginning of the twentieth century there were scarcely more than 1100 British civil servants in the whole of India. These civil servants were often ignorant of local conditions. They always relied on minor Indian officials to carry out the routine of day-to-day administration (No 10). Far from being an agent of change, the British civil servant in India was more often than not a prisoner of local conditions (No 11).

Viewed in these terms, the 'Age of Reform' is probably a myth. Some things changed but many more remained the same. The coins used by the East India Company bore the image, not of the British monarch, but of the Mughal emperor. The emperor had little authority but he still occupied his throne at Delhi. He was important as a symbol of Indian government. It is significant that the British did not see fit to depose him until the end of the rebellion in India in 1858. In the same way, the courts introduced by the British continued to apply Hindu and Muslim laws in reaching their decisions. Despite the work of missionaries, the British were responsible in several places for the upkeep of Hindu temples. *Sati* might have been outlawed but this did not mean that it was no longer practised. How could the British enforce it? In any case, the law against *sati* was introduced only because it had the support of a number of Hindu social and religious reformers, like Rammohan Roy (No 12).

It was the same story with education and communications. By the middle of the nineteenth century about 200 British schools and colleges provided Western education for

3.1 John Bull converting the Indians, an illustration from Qui Hi, a satirical poem published in 1816. The poem criticised the British for their lack of respect towards Indian customs. In this illustration, John Bull is shown as an absentee landlord. After taking rent from the Indians, he threatens to force the Bible on the Muslim (seated with hands clasped), the Parsee (standing) and the Hindu Brahmin.

a mere 30,000 Indian students. Only 34 miles of railway line had been constructed, although communications had been improved by the laying of some 4000 miles of telegraph lines. Education and railways did not produce significant results until the second half of the nineteenth century. Judith Brown, one of the new generation of British historians of India, has written of the early nineteenth century: 'An age of reform existed in the minds of many of the British concerned with India: whether it ever existed in Indians' experience is doubtful.' (*Modern India: The Making of an Asian Democracy*, Cambridge, 1985, page 81). Why, then, was there a rebellion in India in 1857? This question is examined in the next chapter.

THE DEBATE ABOUT INDIA

1. The views of a Conservative. Sir John Malcolm, Indian administrator, Governor of Bombay 1826–30, giving evidence before a House of Commons Select Committee of Enquiry into the affairs of the East India Company, 17 April 1832

Our geat error in India appears to have been a desire to establish systems founded on general principles ... that were often in advance of many of the communities for whose benefit they were intended ... In our precipitate [hurried] attempts to improve the condition of the people, we have often proceeded without sufficient knowledge ... I have been led, by what I have seen, to apprehend as much danger from political as from religious zealots [extremists]. If the latter at times create alarm to the natives from infringing their superstitious observances and religion, the former unsettle their minds by the introduction of principles and forms of administration foreign to their usage ... We should proceed with much caution, for the natives never appear to forget that we are strangers ...

2. A warning against missionaries. Thomas Twining, who had worked in India, in a letter to the Chairman of the Court of Directors of the East India Company, 1807

I will venture to say, that there is not, in the world, a people more jealous and tenacious of their religious opinions and ceremonies, than the native inhabitants of the East. Sir, the people of India are not a political, but a religious people. In this respect they differ, I fear, from the inhabitants of this country. They think as much of their Religion, as we of our Constitution ... As long as we continue to govern India in the mild and tolerant spirit of Christianity, we may govern it with ease: but if ever the fatal day shall arrive, when religious innovation shall set her foot in that country, indignation will spread from one end of Hindostan to the other; and the arms of fifty millions of people will drive us from that portion of the globe, with as much ease as the sand of the desert is scattered by the wind.

3. The views of a Utilitarian. James Mill, Examiner of Correspondence at East India House 1819–36, giving evidence before a House of Commons Select Committee of Enquiry into the affairs of the East India Company, 16 February 1832

In my opinion the best thing for the happiness of the people is, that our government should be nominally, as well as really, extended over those territories; that our own mode of governing should be adopted, and our own people put in charge of the government ... The mass of the people, I believe, care very little by what sort of persons they are governed ... they are equally contented whether their comfort is under rulers with turbans or hats.

4. *The views of an Evangelical. Speech by William Wilberforce, the anti-slave trade campaigner and a leading Evangelical, 1813*

[L]et us endeavour to strike our roots into the soil by the gradual introduction and establishment of our own principles and opinions; of our laws, institutions, and manners; above all, as the source of every other improvement, of our religion, and consequently of our morals ... Are we so little aware of the vast superiority even of European laws and institutions, and far more of British institutions, over those of Asia, as not to be prepared to predict with confidence, that the Indian community which should have exchanged its dark and bloody superstitions for the genial influence of Christian light and truth, would have experienced such an increase of civil order and security, of social pleasures and domestic comforts, as to be desirous of preserving the blessings it should have acquired; and can we doubt that it would be bound even by the ties of gratitude to those [the British] who have been the honoured instruments of communicating them?

5. *The views of a Free Trader. Pamphlet written by J Lester, one of the East India Company's engineers in India, 1813*

The vast peninsula of India has for centuries been harassed by wars and devastation, rendering property very insecure; but if it becomes open to a free trade, under one mild, liberal, and effective government that could protect the property, laws, lives and liberties of the subjects, what a sudden change we might not anticipate? We should not only see the palaces of the *Rajah* [prince], and the houses of the *Vakeels* [lawyers], *Aumils* [revenue or rent collectors], *Shrofs* [bankers], and *Zemindars* [landlords], furnished and decorated with the produce of English arts and manufactures, but the *Ryots* [peasants], who form so large a part of the Indian population, may, like the British farmers, have a taste for foreign produce, as soon as they can acquire property enough to procure [obtain] it ... Under these circumstances a trade might suddenly grow beyond the Cape of Good Hope, to take off all the surplus manufactures that Britain can produce.

THE LAW AGAINST *SATI*

6. *Minute by Lord Bentinck, Governor-General of India, 8 November 1829*

The first and primary object of my heart is the benefit of the Hindus. I know nothing so important to the improvement of their future condition as the establishment of a purer morality, whatever their belief, and a more just conception of the will of God. The first step to this better understanding will be dissociation of religious belief and practice from blood and murder. They will then, when no longer under this brutalising excitment, view with more calmness acknowledged truths ... I disown in these remarks, or in this measure, any view whatever to conversion to our own faith. I write and feel as a legislator for the Hindus, and as I believe many enlightened Hindus think and feel.

NOTE: Meaning 'devoted', *sati* was supposed to be a voluntary act whereby the Hindu widow rejoined her god-husband through the flames of purity. In practice it was usually forced upon her by relatives who were anxious for the presige of a *sati* in the family, greedy for her possessions, or simply wanting one less mouth to feed. *Sati* represented a corrupt form of Hinduism. It was an ancient custom but not one that was sanctioned by the Vedas, the oldest Hindu scriptures. Nor was it widely practised, being restricted mainly to the highest castes.

THE INTRODUCTION OF WESTERN EDUCATION INTO INDIA

7. *Lord Macaulay's Minute on Education in India, 2 February 1835*

I have no knowledge of either Sanskrit or Arabic. But I have done what I could to form a correct estimate of their value. I have read translations of the most celebrated Arabic and Sanskrit works. I have conversed both here and at home with men distinguished by their proficiency in the Eastern tongues. I am quite ready to take the Oriental learning at the valuation of the Orientalists themselves. I have never found one among them who could deny that a single shelf of a good European library was worth the whole native literature of India and Arabia. The intrinsic superiority of the Western literature is, indeed, fully admitted by those members of the Committee who support the Oriental plan of education ... In one point I fully agree with the gentlemen to whose general views I am opposed. I feel with them, that it is impossible for us, with our limited means to attempt to educate the body of the people. We must do our best to form a class who may be interpreters between us and the millions whom we govern; a class of persons, Indian in blood and colour, but English in taste, in opinions, in morals, and in intellect.

8. *Lord Macaulay on 'the proudest day in English history', from a speech in July 1833*

It may be that the public mind of India may expand under our system till it has outgrown that system; that by good government we may educate our subjects into a capacity for better government; that having become instructed in European knowledge, they may, in some future age, demand European institutions. Whether such a day will come I know not. But never will I attempt to avert or retard it. Whenever it comes, it will be the proudest day in English history. To have found a great people sunk in the lowest depths of slavery and superstition, to have so ruled them as to have made them desirous and capable of all the privileges of citizens, would indeed be a title to glory all our own.

9. *Extract from 'The Education of the People of India' by Charles Edward Trevelyan, 1838. Trevelyan was Macaulay's young brother-in-law. He occupied a number of senior government positions in an Indian career stretching from 1827–1865*

The existing connection between two such distant countries as England and India, cannot, in the nature of things, be permanent: no effort of policy can prevent the natives from ultimately regaining their independence. But there are two ways of arriving at this point. One of these is through the medium of revolution; the other, through that of reform ... The only means at our disposal for preventing the one and securing the other class of results is, to set the natives on a process of European improvement, to which they are already sufficiently inclined. They will then cease to desire and aim at independence on the old Indian footing ... The political education of a nation is a work of time; and while it is in progress, we shall be as safe as it will be possible for us to be. The natives will not rise against us, we shall stoop to raise them; there will be no reaction, because there will be no pressure; the national activity will be be fully and harmlessly employed in acquiring and diffusing [spreading] European knowledge ...

THE LIMITED IMPACT OF BRITISH RULE

10. *Sir Thomas Munro, Governor of Madras 1820–1827, writing in 1817*

Where there is no village establishment, we have no hold upon the people, no means of acting upon them, none of establishing confidence. Our situation, as foreigners, renders a regular village establishment [of Indian officials] more important to us than to a native [Indian] Government: our inexperience, and our ignorance of the circumstances of the people, make it more necessary for us to seek the aid of regular establishments to direct the internal affairs of the country, and our security requires that we should have a body of head men of villages interested in supporting our dominion.

11. *Alexander Walker, British Resident at Baroda, commenting on the influence of a minor Indian official in neighbouring Bombay, 1820*

[A]lmost every European servant has a favourite native, and it is astonishing what power and ascendancy he soon obtains. These Native favourites are generally men of low origin, tho of great shrewdness, without much education but possess of ... strong natural endowments [qualities] ... Through this medium the European gentleman is never well informed, and the [Indian village] inhabitant who has no other channel of justice, or means of obtaining redress for his injuries, soon gives up the pursuit and submits in silence.

12. Hindu support for the law against sati. Extract from a letter written by Rammohan Roy in 1832. For more about Rammohan Roy, see chapter 6

Though it is impossible for a thinking man not to feel the evils of political subjection and dependence on a foreign people, yet when we reflect on the advantages which we have derived and may hope to derive from our connection with Great Britain, we may be reconciled to the present state of things which promises permanent benefits to our prosperity. Besides security from foreign invaders and internal plunderers, let us ask ourselves, whether we could have rescued ourselves from the stigma of female murder ... but for the English?

CHAPTER FOUR

THE REBELLION OF 1857 IN INDIA

Contrasting views of the Rebellion

In April 1857 eighty-five sepoys at the garrison town of Meerut to the north-east of Delhi refused to use greased cartridges which had been issued with the new Enfield rifle. This act of defiance acted as the spark for one of the most controversial episodes in Indian history. Some have described the events of 1857 simply as an army mutiny. Others have described them as a nationalist uprising or as a war of indpendence. Another view suggests that the truth lies somewhere between these two, and that the events of 1857 represented something more more than a mutiny but less than a war of independence.

The Sepoy Revolt

Of the many causes of the rebellion, the military mutiny by the sepoys is perhaps the easiest to explain. Sepoy comes from the Hindi word *sipahi*, meaning soldier. Sepoys served in large numbers in the three armies maintained by the East India Company in India – the Bengal Army, the Bombay Army and the Madras Army. The mutiny of 1857 was confined to the Bengal Army which was the largest of the three. Hindus and Muslims served in the Bengal Army. The sepoys came from many different parts of northern India. One-third came from Oudh, an Indian kingdom which the British had annexed in 1856. Most of the Hindus in the Bengal Army were of high caste. For Hindus, military service came after teaching religion as the most honourable profession. The sepoys in the Bengal Army had many grievances over their conditions of service. In particular, they resented the loss of their extra field allowance for 'foreign' service. This allowance had been paid to them when they campaigned within India but hundreds of miles from their home territory. As more of India came under British rule, the British regarded all postings within India as home service. The extra field allowance was therefore abolished. A number of regiments of the Bengal Army had mutinied in the 1840s when sent on campaigns without the field allowance. The sepoys were also expected to serve overseas. Travel by sea was considered polluting by high caste Hindus. It was forbidden by their religion and they faced being disowned by their families and communities.

The sepoy in the Bengal Army was therefore likely to be very suspicious if his caste or religion seemed under threat. The cartridges issued with the new Enfield rifle in 1857 presented a new threat. They were greased with beef and pork fat, contaminating to Hindus and Muslims respectively. The tip of the cartridge had to be bitten off before it could be loaded into the rifle (No 1). The British realised the problem and issued new loading instructions which avoided the need to bite the cartridges. But it was too late; the damage had been done. Some of the sepoys clearly felt that their religion was in danger (No 2). Given that so many came from Oudh, they were also likely to be bitter about that kingdom's annexation in 1856 (No 3).

The grievances of the sepoys were only one aspect of the military revolt. The other was British military weakness. Of 150,000 men in the Bengal Army, only 23,000 were British (No 4). This was partly because a number of British regiments had been withdrawn in 1853 to fight in the Crimean War. In 1857, British troops were concentrated in Bengal (the centre of British power in India) and in the Punjab (annexed at the end of the 1840s). In between – throughout the North-Western Provinces and Oudh, the strongholds of the rebellion (fig 4.1) – there were hardly any British troops at all (No 5).

The Civilian Revolt

The rebellion of 1857 was not simply a military mutiny. Civil unrest was also widespread. Accounting for this is rather more difficult. From Meerut, the sepoys marched on Delhi, the old Mughal capital. Here they persuaded Bahadur Shah, the last of the Mughal emperors, to act as a rallying point for the rebellion. Bahadur Shah was a frail old man of eighty-two. He was taken by surprise and had no option but to agree. In August 1857 a proclamation listing Indian grievances was issued in the name of the Emperor (No 6). Intended to rally popular support, it is perhaps questionable whether the proclamation can be regarded as a reliable guide to the feelings of the people. In 1858, when the rebellion was over, Syed Ahmed Khan wrote an essay on its causes. The author, a Muslim, had worked for the East India Company and he supported the British. His essay was the most important Indian contribution to the debate about the nature of the rebellion. An English translation of the Urdu original was published soon after.

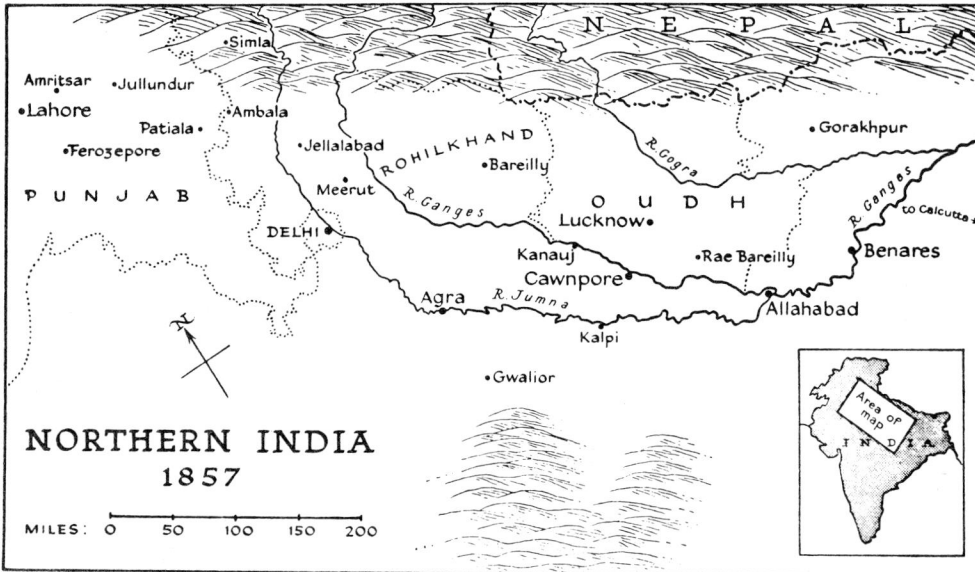

4.1 Map of Northern India, 1857, showing the key areas of the Rebellion.

Syed Ahmed Khan believed that the rebellion had been caused by ignorance – ignorance on the part of the people about the government's intentions, and ignorance on the part of the government about the condition of the people. As a remedy, he suggested that the government should take steps to consult Indian opinion (No 7).

The Indian leaders

On the Indian side, the rebellion produced some notable leaders, like Nana Saheb and the *rani* or queen of Jhansi. They became famous as symbols of Indian resistance to foreign rule. Both had lost their kingdoms to the British. Nana Saheb was a descendant of the Peshwa, the Maratha leader defeated by the British at the beginning of the nineteenth century. Hated by the British because of the massacre at Cawnpore (figs 4.2 and 4.3), Nana Saheb escaped from India at the end of the rebellion and died in exile in Nepal. The kingdom of Jhansi, another Maratha state, had been annexed by the British in 1854 when the male ruler died without a natural heir. In June 1857 the European residents of the

4.2 An artist's impression of the massacre which took place at Cawnpore in June and July 1858. The town of Cawnpore (now Kanpur) was besieged by sepoys acting on the instructions of Nana Saheb in June 1858. The British garrison, which included women and children as well as troops, surrendered. After negotiations, the British were given safe conduct to leave Cawnpore unharmed. Boats were provided to take them down river to Allahabad. As they were about to leave, a signal was given and they were shot down from all sides. The survivors, about 200 women and children, were imprisoned on Nana Saheb's orders. But an order went out that they too should be killed. The sepoys refused to kill them and so butchers were sent in with knives. The women and children were hacked to death and their remains thrown down a well.

town of Jhansi were massacred by the sepoys of the local garrison. The British decided that the *rani* was personally responsible but it is now generally agreed that she was innocent. Because of British hostility, she had no option but to join the rebel armies. She took back her kingdom but was killed in battle in 1858 (No 8).

4.3 The Rebellion witnessed acts of great savagery and cruelty on both sides. This particular form of execution was deliberately chosen by the British to torment the victims after death. The sepoys believed that there could be no peace after death if the body was incomplete. They were sent into perpetual misery when their bodies were blown to pieces from the mouths of cannons. The British were in no mood to show mercy. General Neil, a British officer, led a relief force to Cawnpore which arrived too late to prevent the massacre. Upon arrival he gave orders that those responsible for the deaths of the women and children should be made to clean up the building in which the massacre had taken place. They were made to lick the blood from the walls and then hanged. On his march to Cawnpore, before he knew about the massacre, Neil had created a reign of terror in the surrounding countryside. Sepoys were hanged indiscriminately and villages were burnt. The British had begun to take their revenge for the Rebellion even before an incident such as the Cawnpore massacre became widely known.

The grievances of the landlords

Within the countryside at large, the rebellion was led by once-powerful landlords. Known as *taluqdars* in the North-Western Provinces and Oudh and *zamindars* elsewhere, these landlords were said to have many grievances against the British. The argument runs something like this. The landlords had land taken away from them by the British when they could not provide documents or title-deeds proving that they owned their land. For the British, the land was their main source of income. Each landlord payed rent to the government, calculated upon the basis of what his land was worth and the crops grown.

Many landlords claimed that they were being asked to pay too much. They had to borrow from money-lenders and some were forced to sell land to pay off their debts. The courts which the British introduced always seemed to side with the money-lenders when debt cases were brought before them. The British certainly dealt roughly with some of these landlords. They regarded them as parasites on the land who took money which rightfully belonged to the government. Outside Bengal, where the landlords had recognised rights, the British wanted to eliminate these 'middle-men' and deal direct with the peasants. Industrious and hard-working, the peasants were said to be the people with a genuine interest in improving the land. If more land was brought under cultivation and more crops were grown, the government would be able to claim a higher share of the proceeds.

This argument sounds a convincing explanation of landlord revolt, but is it supported by the evidence? Many landlords who lost land were to the forefront of the rebellion (No 9) but others in the same position remained passive and in some cases actually supported the British (No 10). What appears to be a contradiction is in fact evidence of just how difficult it is to be precise about the causes of the rebellion. Equally, some of the disturbances in the countryside were not directed against the British. As law and order broke down, different caste groups and clans took the opportunity to settle old scores with each other (No 11). It was often the case that if one caste group rebelled, the rival group supported the British.

The nature of the Rebellion and the reasons why it failed

Various explanations have been put forward to explain why the rebellion failed (Nos 12–13). Similarly, different views have been put forward to explain what the rebellion represented. For some it was a nationalist struggle and a war of independence (No 14); for others it represented something much less (No 15). The revolt did not have the support of all Indians. The Sikhs of the Punjab did not rebel (No 15) and most of the Indian princes supported the British. It was also noticeable that areas which had been longest exposed to British influence, such as Bengal, remained quiet (No 16).

The consequences of the Rebellion

No less significant than its causes were the consequences of the rebellion. The East India Company was abolished and India taken under direct British rule. The rebellion shook the British but they came out of it convinced that what they were doing in India was right. If the rebellion taught them anything, it was that they had been going about it in the wrong way (No 17). Reform of the army was given priority. The ratio of Indian to British troops was fixed at 2:1 and new Indian recruits were drawn from races which had stayed loyal, such as the Sikhs and the Gurkhas. The racial composition of Indian Army regiments was now based on the principle of divide and rule (No 18). Attitudes towards the Indian princely kingdoms were reversed. The British now decided that it was in their interests to have the support of the princes. Kingdoms were no longer annexed when a prince died without a natural heir. Instead, the princes were permitted to adopt successors. Attitudes towards the landlords were reversed in the same way and for the same reason (No 19). The rebellion did not alter the government's views about the need for Western education. Educated people were thought to make loyal subjects and popular ignorance was regarded as a source of political danger (No 20). However, in other areas, for instance religion and social customs, the British realised that they would have to tread very carefully (No 21). The British 'civilising' mission in India was now defined as one of providing law and order and good government. It would be a long time before Indians became capable of governing themselves (No 22). Finally, at the level of race relations, the rebellion made matters much worse. British settlers in India began to think and act like a community living under siege conditions. Equality was ruled out. The British believed in white superiority and racism reared its ugly head in a more extreme form (Nos 23–24).

THE SEPOY REVOLT

1. General Anson, Commander-in-Chief, Ambala, to the Governor-General, Lord Canning, 23 March 1857

I am not so much surprised at their [the sepoys'] objections to the cartridges, having seen them. I had no idea they contained, or rather are smeared with, such a quantity of grease, which looks exactly like fat. After ramming down the ball, the muzzle of the musket is covered with it.

2. Sir Henry Lawrence, Chief Commissioner of Oudh, to Lord Canning, 9 May 1857

Last night I had a conversation with a *Jumadar* [a junior officer] of the Oude Artillery for more than one hour, and was startled by the dogged persistence of the man – a Brahmin of about forty years of age and of excellent character – in the belief that for ten years past [the] Government had been engaged in measures for the forcible or rather fraudulent conversion of all Natives.

3. Bishop Heber's account of a conversation during his journey through the kingdom of Oudh in 1825

I asked also if the people thus oppressed desired, as I had been assured they did, to be placed under English government. Captain Lockitt said that he had heard the same thing; but on his way this year to Lucknow, and conversing, as his admirable knowledge of Hindoostanee enables him to do, familiarly with the *suwarrs* [cavalrymen] who accompanied him, and who spoke out, like all the rest of their countrymen, on the weakness of the king and the wickedness of the government, he fairly put the question to them, when the *Jemautdar* [junior officer], joining his hands, said, with great fervency, 'Miserable as we are, of all miseries keep us from that!'. 'Why so?', said Captain Lockitt, 'are not our people far better governed?'. 'Yes', was the answer, 'but the name of Oude and the honour of our nation would be at an end'.

BRITISH MILITARY WEAKNESS

4. Sir John Lawrence, Chief Commissioner of the Punjab, to Sir Charles Trevelyan, 16 December 1857

The cartridge question was to my mind, indubitably, the immediate cause of the revolt. But the army had for a long time been in an unsatisfactory state. It had long seen and felt its power. We had gone on, year by year, adding to its numbers, without adding to our European force ... The Bengal army was one of great brotherhood, in which all the members felt and acted in union.

5. Martin Richard Gubbins, Financial Commissioner of Oudh, writing in 1858

All the causes, however, which have been enumerated, might have been in operation, and yet would have failed to produce the mutiny, but for the capital error which was committed, of denuding our provinces of European troops. Religious alarm might have been excited; the native soldier might have been at the same time discontented and insubordinate; the *talooqdars* of Oudh, and the royal families of Delhi and Lucknow might have plotted; yet had we possessed a few English regiments in the country, discontent would never have matured into rebellion. As it was, it may almost be said that there were no European troops ... All our principal cities were without European troops. There were none at Delhi, or at Bareilly; none at Fyzabad, at Mirzapoor, or at Benares. And worst of all, the important fortress of Allahabad, the key of the North-Western Provinces, was equally unprotected! ... Throughout the entire province of Oudh, we possessed but one English battery of artillery: all the rest were native! This absence of European troops was the one, great, capital error.

THE CIVILIAN REBELLION

6. *Proclamation issued in the name of the King of Delhi (Bahadur Shah), 25 August 1857*

It is well known to all, that in this age the people of Hindostan, both Hindoos and Mohammedans, are being ruined under the tyranny and oppression of the infidel and treacherous English ...

Section I. Regarding *Zemindars* [landlords]. It is evident that the British government, in making *zemindary* [land] settlements, have imposed exorbitant *jummas* [rent demands], and have disgraced and ruined several *zemindars* by putting up their estates to public auction for arrears of rent ...

Section II. Regarding Merchants. It is plain that the infidel and treacherous British government have monopolised the trade of all the fine and valuable merchandise, such as indigo, cloth, and other articles of shipping, leaving only the trade of trifles to the people ...

Section III. Regarding Public Servants. It is not a secret thing, that under the British government, natives employed in the civil and military services, have little respect, low pay, and no manner of influence; all the posts of dignity ... are exclusively bestowed on Englishmen ...

Section IV. Regarding Artisans. It is evident that the Europeans, by the introduction of English articles into India, have thrown the weavers, the cotton-dressers, the carpenters, the blacksmiths, and the shoemakers, etc., out of employ ... so that every description of native artisan has been reduced to beggary ...

Section V. Regarding *Pundits* [and] *Fakirs* [learned men of religion] and other learned persons. The *pundits* and *fakirs*, being the guardians of the Hindoo and Mohammedan religions respectively, and the Europeans being the enemies of both religions, and as at present a war is raging against the English on account of religion, the *pundits* and *fakirs* are bound to present themselves to me, and take their share in the holy war, otherwise they will stand condemned ...

7. *Syed Ahmed Khan on the causes of the revolt, 1858*

But the greatest mischief lay in this that the people misunderstood the views and the intentions of Government ... At length the Hindustanees fell into the habit of thinking that all the laws were passed with a view to degrade and ruin them, and to deprive them and their fellows of their religion ... Granted that the intentions of Government were excellent, there was no man who could convince the people of it; no one was at hand to correct the errors which they had adopted. And why? Because there was not one of their own number among the members of the Legislative Council. Had there been, these evils that have happened to us, would have been averted. The more one thinks the matter over, the more one is convinced that here we have the one great cause which was the ·origin of all the smaller causes of dissatisfaction ... I do not wish to enter here into the question as to how the ignorant and uneducated natives of Hindustan could be allowed a share in the deliberations of the Legislative Council: or as to how they should be selected to form an assembly like the English Parliament. These are knotty points. All I wish to prove here is that such a step is absolutely necessary, and that the disturbances are due to the neglect of such a measure.

8. *Account of the death of the rani of Jhansi by Colonel G B Malleson, a 19th century British historian*

Amongst the fugitives in the rebel ranks was the resolute woman who, alike in council and on the field, was the soul of the conspirators. Clad in the attire of a man and mounted on horseback, the *rani* of Jhansi might have been seen animating her troops throughout the day. When inch by inch the British troops pressed through the pass, and when reaching its summit Smith ordered the hussars to charge, the *rani* of Jhansi boldly fronted the British horsemen. When her comrades failed her, her horse, in spite of her efforts, carried her along with the others. With them she might have escaped but that her horse, crossing the canal near the cantonment, stumbled and fell. A hussar, close upon her track, ignorant of her sex and her rank, cut her down. She fell to rise no more. That night her devoted followers, determined that the English should not boast that they had captured her even dead, burned the body. Thus died the *rani* of Jhansi ... Whatever her faults may have been in British eyes, her countrymen will ever remember that she was driven by ill-treatment into rebellion, and that she lived and died for her country.

9. *A taluqdar, Raja Hanmant Singh, explains his reasons for supporting the rebellion to Captain L Barrow, Deputy Commissioner of Oudh, June 1857. The Raja had given refuge to Barrow in his fortress at the beginning of the rebellion. When Barrow bid him farewell and asked for his support in crushing the rebellion, the Raja replied:*

Sahib, your countrymen came into this country and drove out our King. You sent your officers round the districts to examine the titles to the estates. At one blow you took from me lands which from time immemorial had been in my family. I submitted. Suddenly misfortune fell upon you. The people of the land rose against you. You came to me whom you had despoiled. I haved saved you. But now – now I march at the head of my retainers to Lakhnao to try and drive you from the country.

10. Loyal taluqdars. Extract from a report by W H Smith, Settlement Officer, Aligarh in the North-Western Provinces, 1874

Scarcely one member of any of the old and powerful families of the district joined in the disturbances: on the contrary, some of these gave what assistance they could with undoubted readiness ... Thakur Gobind Singh, the son of the very man whose fort we had taken and whose power we had crushed ... was eminently loyal. He never hesitated from the first, but aided us with his followers, fought in our battles, and kept order on our behalf. Raja Tikam Singh, the son of Bhagwant Singh, whose independence we had forcibly destroyed, assisted us throughout to the utmost of his ability, though his own power had been largely reduced by the policy pursued at the last settlement by Mr Thornton.

11. Settling of old scores. Report by E J Boldero, District Collector of Revenue in the North-Western Provinces, December 1858

In this District there seems to have been no such thing as a national attempt at the subversion of Government authority. No sooner did the mutiny commence, the Ahir tribe resumed their predatory [plundering] habits and were followed by the Chowhan Rajpoots ... All restraints were cast off and every malcontent found an opportunity for avenging old wrongs or recovering former possessions. Then followed the struggle for mastery between these two tribes, and ended in the subversion of the Ahirs by the Chowhans. It was owing in great measure to these incessant commotions that so many estates were plundered, and the prevalence of anarchy and suspension of authority were prolonged for so long a period.

THE FAILURE OF THE REBELLION

12. The views of Hira Lal Gupta, an Indian historian

Inadequate military resources of the rebels was the greatest weakness of India struggling for freedom ... With the exception of personal arms and ammunition and those seized from the Government arsenals and magazines, there was no other source from which modern military equipment ... could be supplied to the people engaged in a deadly struggle. Artillery there was none ... Modern scientific means of communication under British control, like the widespread telegraph system and postal communications, blasted the prospects of success ... The copies of the original telegrams sent from one place to another confirm the importance of the role of the telegraph system in suppressing the uprisings ... The telegraph system served the Governor-General and the

Commander-in-Chief better than their right arms. By it they received information in no time and acted with great promptitude. The return of troops from Persia and the Crimea was hastened. Reinforcements came from Madras, Bombay and Ceylon. The British naval and military expedition on its way to China was intercepted and diverted to India with all possible speed. The march of battalions and movements of artillery could be directed telegraphically.

13. The views of T R Metcalf, an American historian

But in their vision of the future the rebel leaders were hopelessly at odds. They could never agree on what to set in the place of the British Raj. No one conceived of India as an independent state on the European model, and the call for a return to the past only concealed deep and abiding conflicts among them. Some would revive the Mughal Empire; others, the followers of Nana Saheb, dreamed of a new and powerful Maratha state; still others, from the *rani* of Jhansi to the 'King of Fourteen Villages' in Mathura District, celebrated their own independence and prepared to fight against all comers. United in defeat, the rebel leaders would have fallen at each other's throats in victory.

THE CHARACTER OF THE REBELLION

14. Extract from 'The Indian War of Independence of 1857' by V D Savarkar, 1909. Savarkar was a young Indian revolutionary when he wrote this book. He came to London as a student and formed a terrorist organisation. His book on the rebellion was banned by the British government but copies were smuggled into India. Savarkar was clearly writing for a political purpose

What, then, were the real causes and motives of this Revolution? What were they that they could make thousands of heroes unsheath their swords and flash them on the battlefield? What were they that had the power to brighten up pale and rusty crowns and raise from the dust abased flags? What were they that for them men by the thousand willingly poured their blood year after year? ... These great principles were *Swadharma* [a sense of duty] and *Swaraj* [self-government] ... In what other history is the principle of love of one's country manifested more nobly than in ours?

15. The views of R C Majumdar, an Indian historian

In this connection a very important fact is often forgotten by those who claim the outbreak of 1857 as a national war of independence, for which patriotic sepoys shed their blood, and political leaders had been preparing grounds for a long time. The

Punjab was conquered by the British with the help of the sepoys less than ten years before the outbreak of the mutiny ... If there were really a moment for freeing India from the British yoke, obviously this was the most suitable opportunity. But we have not the least evidence to show that the Indian leaders like Nana Saheb and others ... raised their little finger to help the cause of the Sikhs. The sepoys themselves, who are supposed to have sacrificed their all for the sake of their country in 1857, had not the least scruple to fight the Sikhs who were the last defender of liberty in India ... As a matter of fact we can hardly expect a national war of independence in India either in 1857 or at any time before it. For nationalism or patriotism, in the true sense, was conspicuous by its absence in India till a much later date. To regard the outbreak of 1857 as either national in character or a war for independence of India, betrays a lack of true knowledge of the history of the Indian people in the nineteenth century.

16. Resolution passed by the British Indian Association, Calcutta, May 1857

The Committee view with disgust and horror the disgraceful and mutinous conduct of the native soldiery at those stations [Meerut and Delhi], and the excesses committed by them, and confidently trust to find that they have met with no sympathy ... or support from the bulk of the civil population of that part of the country, or from any reputable or influential classes among them.

NOTE: The British Indian Association was founded at Calcutta in 1851. Most of its members were landlords but it also represented traders and men in the professions such as law and journalism who had benefited from Western education.

THE RESULTS OF THE REBELLION

17. Charles Raikes, a District Officer in the North-Western Provinces, on the lesson to be learned, 1858

Our intentions towards India have generally been well inspired, but the fatal error of attempting to force the policy of Europe on the people of Asia which has hitherto ... pervaded our Indian history both military and civil, must be corrected for the future, as it has been atoned for in the past.

18. Sir Charles Wood, Secretary of State for India, to Lord Canning, 8 April 1861

I hold most strongly to having the three separate armies, with as little connection between them as possible. Indeed, I am for raising Regiments, that is, recruiting them, from separate Districts, so that, though the men of a Regiment should be neighbours or cousins when at home, there should be as little connection as possible between different

Regiments. I never wish to see again a great Army, very much the same in its feelings and prejudices and connections, confident in its strength, and so disposed to unite in rebellion *together*. If one regiment mutinies, I should like to have the next so alien that it would be ready to fire into it.

19. *Charles Raikes on the treatment of taluqdars, 1858*

How then are we to treat the *Talookdars* in the future? I can only suggest that without compromising the rights of our humbler and weaker subjects in Oude, we should let the *Talookdar* down easily, and treat him not only with justice but liberality. The extinction of this class of men is not consistent with the safety or durability of our empire, we have erred, with the best possible intentions, in paying too little heed to the position of the landed aristocracy, and our best plan is to acknowledge our error and to retrieve it.

20. *F J Halliday, Lieutenant-Governor of Bengal, on the future of Western education in India, January 1860*

I do not think it possible ... in any ... part of the world, European or Asiatic, to inaugurate, however cautiously, a system of education for a people yet wholly ignorant and benighted [uneducated], without exciting suspicion, or disatisfaction, or both. Nor do I believe that your benighted European peasant is a bit easier to exalt than his Hindoo brother ... or at all less jealous and suspicious when his prejudices are attacked or interfered with. But what then? Are we to stay our healing hand because the patient is ignorant and refractory [stubborn]. The condition of popular ignorance is everywhere the condition of political danger, and for that reason alone we ought to persevere in our endeavours to remove it.

21. *Sir Charles Wood, Secretary of State for India, speaking in the House of Commons, August 1859*

We learn first of all that we must be very careful not to give to the Natives of India any reason to believe that we are about to attack the religious feelings and prejudices which they hold so dear. No doubt in the recent case there was no just cause for suspicion; but they entertained that belief. We have seen the consequences, and if we hope to retain India in peace and tranquillity we must take care so to govern it as not only to consult the interests, but the feelings of the Native population.

22. *Sir John Strachey, a member of the Viceroy's Council, writing in 1884*

When we say that we cannot always in our Government of India ignore differences of race, this is only another way of saying that the English in India are a handful of foreigners governing 250 millions of people. Although I suppose that no foreign government was ever accepted with less repugnance than that with which the British Government is accepted in India, the fact remains that there has never been a country, and never will be, in which the government of foreigners is really popular. It will be the beginning of the end of our empire when we forget this elementary fact, and entrust the greater executive power to the hands of natives, on the assumption that they will always be faithful and strong supporters of our government. In this there is nothing offensive or disparaging to the natives of India. It simply means that we are foreigners and that not only in our own interests but because it is our highest duty towards India itself, we intend to maintain our dominion. We cannot foresee the time in which the cessation of our rule would not be the signal for universal anarchy and ruin, and it is clear that the only hope for India is the long continuance of the benevolent but strong government of Englishmen.

23. Speech by Sir Mordaunt Wells, a British planter in India, in the Indian Legislative Council, June 1860. Wells was taking part in a debate about a new law which was designed to restrict the possession of firearms (shotguns and pistols) in India. He argued that the law should not apply to Europeans

Did the conduct of the Europeans during the mutiny, when the life of every European in the country was in jeopardy – and there could be no doubt that on that occasion it was a struggle on the part of the native races to exterminate Europeans in this country – did the conduct of Europeans afford any justification for the change? ... On what ground then was the measure based? Was it on the ground of expediency? Was it on the ground of equality? There was no equality, as late events had shown, when Europeans had to defend their lives against hordes of natives. It was not a matter of English feeling – it was a matter of strict justice ... There could be no equality in treating Europeans, of whose loyalty there was never any suspicion, on the same terms, with regard to this question, as natives.

24. Sir George Clarke, Governor of Bombay, to Lord Morley, Secretary of State for India, December 1907

[I]f we could ensure that no civilian, or soldier, or globetrotter should ever come to India without having the duty of courteous treatment of natives driven into his skull, some of our difficulties would, in time, disappear. Undoubtedly there is too much harshness of words and acts, unconscious perhaps, but none the less galling for that reason. I suppose the theory is that the dominant race, being dependent on force and in a hopeless numerical minority, must assert itself ...

CHAPTER FIVE

THE INDIAN ECONOMY
UNDER BRITISH RULE:
EXPLOITATION OR DEVELOPMENT?

Contrasting views about the effects of British rule

It is unlikely that historians will ever agree about the effects of British rule on the Indian economy. Extracts 1–2 indicate how widely opinions differ. However, it would be wrong to assume that the British and Indians always lined up on opposite sides of the argument. During British times, there were always those Indians who were ready to accept that in a number of ways India had benefited under British rule. Equally, there were always those British people who were self-critical and who were ready to admit that in certain respects British rule had been damaging to the Indian economy. The same is true today as British and Indian economic historians survey the evidence.

Karl Marx on India

A useful starting point is to consider what Karl Marx said about India. Marx studied colonial economies as well as those in Europe which were in the first stages of industrialisation. He believed that Britain had a double role in India and that the development of railways would lead to an industrial revolution (No 3). The railways in India certainly grew at an impressive rate (No 4). By 1910, India had the fourth largest railway network in the world. But the industrial revolution which Marx predicted did not happen. When India became independent in 1947, she ranked as an underdeveloped country and one of the poorest in the world.

Why was this? Was it because of British exploitation, the backwardness of the Indian economy (as suggested by some of the extracts in chapter 1), or because of certain other factors? The remaining extracts in this chapter consider the development of the colonial economy in India.

India as a market for British goods: The Textile Trade

India was an important market or sales area for British goods, particularly cotton textiles. It was also an area of investment for British capital or money (No 5). The Indian nationalists complained that imports of British cotton goods from the mills of Lancashire had all but wiped out the handloom industry in India (Nos 6–7). They also complained that Britain's tariff or customs policy was unfair because it protected the mills of Lancashire against competition from the new Indian cotton mills at Bombay in Western India. During the second half of the nineteenth century, the Government in Britain supported a policy of free trade. Free trade meant a free exchange of goods between countries without any obstacles in the form of customs duties. But the British Government in India had a different view. The Indian Government was always short of money, largely, as we shall see, because it spent so much on the army. Customs duties were therefore seen by the Indian Government as a means of raising more money. In 1894, a 5 per cent customs duty was imposed on British cotton goods entering India. The mill-owners of Lancashire protested. They said that this would damage their biggest overseas market. The mill-owners had powerful friends in Parliament and the Government in London gave in to their pressure. To balance the 5 per cent duty on British cotton goods, the Government of India was ordered to introduce an excise duty of $3\frac{1}{2}$ per cent on Indian cotton goods. An excise duty is a domestic tax charged on goods for the home market, either when they are being made or before they are sold to home consumers. It therefore became more expensive for the Indian cotton mills to sell their own goods to their own people (No 8).

Foreign Investment in India

The methods of foreign investment in India were criticised by the nationalists. They argued that profits were taken out of the country. Foreigners who invested in Indian railways were guaranteed a 5 per cent dividend or return on their money, irrespective of whether the lines in which they invested showed a profit. The nationalists also complained that too much was spent on railways and not enough on irrigation and education. They argued that more should be spent on irrigation as a means of combating famines (Nos 9–11). Equally, they did not regard India's growing population as the main reason why famines caused so much distress (Nos 12–13).

The 'Drain of Wealth'

To the nationalists, the methods of investment in India were part of a much wider process which they described as the 'drain of wealth'. The 'Home Charges' were the most significant aspect of this drain. These charges represented money paid each year by India to Britain. Some of the money took the form of interest payments on loans which were used to build railways and to dig canals. The money also included payments for what were known as services and stores. Payments for services covered the costs of British administration. These costs included the salaries of British civil servants working in India, the pensions of those civil servants who had retired, money spent on keeping British troops in India and money spent on running the India Office in London. The India Office was the government department responsible for Indian affairs. India paid the wages of everyone who worked at the India Office – from the Secretary of State, the minister in charge, at the top, to the cleaning ladies at the bottom. Payments for stores covered the cost of equipment and machinery – from typewriters to railway coaches – which were used by the government departments in India. Most of the stores were purchased from Britain. The total cost of the Home Charges rose from £18.9 million over the period 1889–1914, to £28 million in 1933–34. It was a matter of opinion as to which country – India or Britain – benefited most from the services and stores paid for out of these Home Charges (No 14).

Military Expenditure

The vast sums of money which were spent on administration and defence caused particular resentment in India (No 15). Defence spending was so high because India paid the entire cost of two armies – the Indian Army itself and the British Army in India. The ratio between the two armies was 2:1. This was a consequence of the Rebellion of 1857 in India after which the British decided that there should be one British soldier in India for every two Indian soldiers. The strength of the Indian Army in 1880 was 135,000; that of the British Army in India 65,000. It was more expensive to maintain British troops. Indians were not allowed to hold commissions in the army (i.e. to become officers) until the twentieth century and this too added to the expense. It was not only the nationalists who complained about the burden of military expenditure (fig 5.1). In this, and other respects, India was much worse off than other countries which were part of the British Empire (No 16).

Published and Distributed on behalf of the people of India by the British Indian Association and the Indian Association of Calcutta, the Bombay Presidency Association, the Sarvajanik Sabha of Poona, the Mahajan Sabha of Madras, the Sind Sabha of Kurrachee and the Praja–hita–Vardhak Sabha of Surat.

INDIAN LEAFLETS. No. 11.

The Appalling Costliness of the Indian Army!!!

"If we turn to a consideration of our expenditure it is to be observed that, owing to the poverty of the people and their consequent inability to bear taxation, the Government of India is unable to supply the funds required for the most necessary and desirable objects."

"It is also to be observed—and that point should never be forgotten in any comprehensive view of questions of Indian polity—that however sound may be the condition of Indian finance, if we look merely to the figures of revenue and expenditure either in the past or present, the economic condition of the people of India, upon whose prosperity the continued soundness of the financial position must ultimately rest, is not altogether satisfactory."

"The poverty of the people of India is a fact which is notorious.

That poverty is abundantly attested by the prevailing low rate of wages, by the statistics which show the pressure of the population on the soil, by the absence of accumulated capital, and by the rough calculation which has recently been made that the average income per head of population is only Rs. 27 a year." (Despatch No. 247 of the Government of India to the Secretary of State, dated Simla, 2nd September 1882.)

LOOK AT THESE FIGURES AND THOSE!

1. Is it just that poor as India is, it should be unwillingly made to pay for the maintenance of a force of 1,90,000 soldiers, of whom 1,25,000 are Indians, at the **extravagant cost of £90 for each combatant**, when the Six Great Powers of Europe, with armies 15¼ times larger in number, obtain the services of a soldier at an average cost of only £33 per annum ! In other words **it costs India 273 per cent.** more per annum for the keep of a soldier than it costs on an average one of the Great Powers of Europe. Remember also that in reality **each British Soldier in India costs nearly £200** per annum or nearly 600 per cent. more than in Europe.

2. Look at this table and ponder well over India's Military Expenditure :—

Annual Cost of EACH SOLDIER in India compared with that obtaining in the Army of the Six Great Powers of Europe.

Countries	Army in Thousands	Gross Annual Expenditure in Millions £	Annual Cost of each Soldier £	Remarks
INDIA	190	17	90	Of these only 64,000 are Europeans; the rest are Native troops.
United Kingdom*	183	16	90	
France†	524	28	54	
Germany†	449	16	35	
Russia†	729	19	26	
Austria†	272	12	47	
Italy†	750	16	21	

* Statistical Abstract for the United Kingdom from 1870 to 1884. Thirty Second Number.
† Statesman's year Book of Facts. (1885.)

5.1 In the autumn of 1885 a delegation from India visited Britain to present India's case at the November general election. They brought with them a manifesto entitled 'Appeal on Behalf of the People of India to the Electors of Great Britain and Ireland', which outlined India's grievances. The manifesto was distributed together with fourteen leaflets, each of which made a specific complaint. Reproduced here are extracts from the leaflet complaining about the cost of the Indian Army.

Industrialisation in India

Finally, it is worth noting that India was not totally without industries when the British left in 1947 (No 17). However, the vast majority of the population was still employed in agriculture and India's industries were limited in terms of what they produced (Nos 18–19). Comparisons have been made between India's slow rate of industrial growth and the rapid rates of growth achieved by Japan and Russia. In the late nineteenth century, the economies of Japan and Russia, like that of India, were largely agricultural. But by the 1930s, Japan and Russia had become major industrial powers. There was an important difference between India on the one hand and Japan and Russia on the other. India was ruled by a foreign power; Japan and Russia were not. In Japan and Russia the state played the most important role in developing new industries. In both cases there was a strong political motive. During the inter-war years, industrial power was seen as the means by which a country could further its territorial ambitions (Japan) or defend itself against attack (Russia). The people, particularly of Stalin's Russia, paid a heavy price as the government's industrial policies were put into practice. In India, by contrast, the state did not play a part in developing new industries. The industries which did emerge were started by Indians working without government support (No 17). The British Government in India was really very conservative and cautious (No 20). It spent most of its money on administration and defence and it was unwilling to make itself even more unpopular by imposing new taxes on the Indian people. In short, there had to be a strong political incentive before a country could launch itself towards rapid industrialisation. In India, the nature of foreign rule meant that this incentive did not exist (No 21).

THE NATURE OF THE DEBATE

1. Romesh Dutt, a nationalist economist, writing in 1901

It is, unfortunately, a fact which no well-informed Indian official will ignore, that, in many ways, the sources of national wealth in India have been narrowed under British rule ... the East India Company and the British Parliament, following the selfish commercial policy of a hundred years ago, discouraged Indian manufacturers in the early years of British rule in order to encourage the rising manufactures of England. Their fixed policy pursued during the last decades of the eighteenth century and the first decades of the nineteenth, was to make India subservient [subordinate] to the industries of Great Britain, and to make the Indian people grow raw produce only, in order to supply material for the looms and manufactories [factories] of Great Britain.

2. Sir John Marriott, a British historian, writing in 1932

British brains, British enterprise, and British capital have, in a material sense, transformed the face of India. Means of communication have been developed: innumerable bridges, over 40,000 miles of railway, 70,000 miles of metalled roads, testify to the skill and industry of British engineers. Irrigation works on a stupendous scale have brought 30,000 acres under cultivation, and thus greatly added to the agricultural wealth of a country which still lives mainly by agriculture. But, on the other hand, the process of industrialisation has already begun. The mills of Bombay have become dangerous competitors to Lancashire, and the Indian jute industry is threatening the prosperity of Dundee. Thanks to improved sanitation ... to a higher standard of living, to irrigation, to canalisation [canal building], to the development of transport, and to carefully thought-out schemes for relief work, famines, which by their regular occurrence formerly presented a perennial problem to humane administrators, have now virtually disappeared. To have conquered the menace of famine ... is a remarkable achievement for which India is wholly indebted to Britain.

WHAT KARL MARX SAID ABOUT INDIA

3. Extract from a letter written in 1853

England has to fulfil a double mission in India: one destructive, the other regenerating – the annihilation of old Asiatic Society, and the laying of the material foundation of western society in Asia ... I know that the English millocracy [the owners of cotton mills] intend to endow [provide] India with railways with the exclusive view of extracting at diminished expenses the cotton and other raw materials for their manufacturers ... But [y]ou cannot maintain a net[work] of railways over an immense country without introducing all those industrial processes necessary to meet the immediate current wants of Railway locomotion. The Railway system will therefore become, in India, truly the forerunner of modern industry.

4. THE GROWTH OF RAILWAYS IN INDIA 1860–1947

1860	1349 kilometres of track
1870	7678
1890	25495
1920–21	56980
1946–47	65217

5. BRITAIN'S ECONOMIC AND FINANCIAL INTERESTS IN INDIA 1870–1913

India's percentage purchases of Britain's total exports

1870–72	8.2	India ranked 3rd among purchasers of British goods
1890–92	12.6	India ranked 2nd
1913	16	India ranked 1st

Exports of British cotton piece-goods in million yards

	Total exports	Exports to India
1880	4496	1813 (40.3%)
1890	5124	2190 (42.7%)
1900	5034	2019 (40.1%)
1913	7075	3000 (42.4%)

British overseas investments in £ million

	Total investments	Investments in India
1870	785	160
1885	1300	270
1913	3780	380

THE IMPORT OF COTTON GOODS FROM BRITAIN

6. R Montgomery Martin, giving evidence before a Select Committee of the House of Commons in 1840. The witness made an independent study of Britain's colonies and spent fourteen months in Bengal between 1829 and 1830

Q. Do you think that British India has suffered in its trade by reason of the commercial regulations adopted and framed by England?

A. ... I have been impressed with the conviction that India has suffered most unjustly in her trade, not merely with England but with all other countries, by reason of the outcry for free trade on the part of England, without permitting to India a free trade herself ... In 1815 the cotton goods exported from India [to England] were 13,000,000 of rupees. In 1832 they were less than 1,000,000. The cotton goods imported into India from England in the same year, 1815, were to the amount of 263,000 crores of rupees; in 1832–33 they were upwards of 4,000,000 ... We have, during the previous quarter of a century, compelled the Indian territories to receive our manufactures; our woollens duty free, our cottons at 2 per cent., and other articles in proportion, while we have continued during that period to levy almost prohibitory duties, or duties varying from 10 to 20, 30, 50, 100, 500 and 1,000 per cent., upon the articles the produce of our own territories; therefore the cry that has taken place for free trade with India, has been a free trade from this country, and not a free trade between India and this country ...

Q. Have the native manufactures of India been, to any extent, superseded [replaced] by British manufactures?

A. By the exportation of our steam-wrought manufactures to India, we not only supplant [replace] the native manufacturer, but also the spinner of twist [thread of cotton fibre] and the grower of cotton. The decay and destruction of Surat, of Dacca, of Moorshedabad, and other places where native manufactures have been carried on, is too painful a fact to dwell on. I do not think that it has been in the fair course of trade; I think it has been the power of the stronger exercised over the weaker.

7. Thomas Cope, a silk-weaver from Macclesfield, giving evidence before the Select Committee, 1840

Q. Do you think that a labourer in this country, who is able to obtain better food than that, has a right to say, we will keep the labourer in the East Indies in that position in which he shall be able to get nothing for his food but rice?

A. I certainly pity the East Indian labourer, but at the same time I have a greater feeling for my own family than I have for the East Indian labourer's family; I think it is wrong to sacrifice the comforts of my family for the sake of the East Indian labourer, because his condition happens to be worse than mine, and I think it is not good legislation to take away our labour and to give it to the East Indian, because his condition is worse than ours. To raise his condition equal to ours, would be to make us destitute of employment [unemployed], and to throw us upon the rest of society to support us by charity, and this I hope will never take place in this country.

THE TARIFF QUESTION

8. Resolution of the Indian National Congress on the 1894 excise duty imposed on Indian cotton goods

(a) That this Congress respectfully enters its emphatic protest against the injustice and impolicy [bad policy] of imposing excise duty on cottons manufactured in British India, as such excise is calculated to cripple seriously the infant mill industry of this country.
(b) That this Congress puts on record its firm conviction that in proposing this excise the interests of India have been sacrificed to those of Lancashire, and strongly deprecates [disapproves of] any such surrender of Indian interests by the Secretary of State ...

FOREIGN INVESTMENT IN INDIA: THE NATIONALIST VIEW OF RAILWAYS

9. *Mr G K Gokhale, giving evidence before the Royal Commission on Expenditure in India, 1897*

At present, owing to the vigorous manner in which railways are constructed, and the way in which foreign capitalists are encouraged to invest their money in India, the result is that we get only the wages of labour, while all the profits that are made there are taken out of the country and our resources are being utilised by others ... I do not mean that the railways themselves are to be condemned – all the railways – but the manner in which the Government are going in for more and more railways, starving more useful things, is an objection; and this has resulted in the exploitation of our resources by the indigo, tea, coffee, and other planters. The policy of free trade has, moreover, been forced upon us too early, thereby destroying all our important industries that existed before, and throwing all the people on the precarious resource of agriculture.

10. *Mr Dinshaw Edulji Wacha, giving evidence before the Royal Commission, 1897*

But I may be permitted to observe that in the present deteriorated condition of Indian agriculture, when there is not enough food grain produced per annum to fully suffice for the entire population, it is of greater importance to construct irrigation works than more railways. It should be remembered that even protective railways against famine, however largely constructed, would give no help to the people in famine stricken districts, whenever a serious famine of the intensity of that now prevailing may occur, if there were not an adequate surplas of grain to carry from one province to another. What is more essential is to stimulate the food supply. Irrigation, therefore, is of infinitely greater importance than railways.

11. *Mr G K Gokhale, giving evidence before the Royal Commission, 1897*

There are more than 537,000 towns and villages in India, with a total population of about 230 millions, and yet there are less than 100,000 public primary schools for them. The population of school-going age in India is about 35 millions, out of whom only about 4 millions ... are under instruction, which means that out of every 100 children of school-going age, 88 are growing up in darkness and ignorance and consequent moral helplessness ... spend more on education for the present, and afterwards on railways.

NOTE: See No 15 below for a percentage breakdown of how money was spent.

FAMINES AND POPULATION

12. *Report of the Indian Famine Commission, 1880*

A main cause of the disastrous consequences of Indian famines, and one of the greatest difficulties in the way of providing relief ... is to be found in the fact that the great mass of the population directly depends on agriculture, and that there is no other industry from which any considerable part of the community derives its support. The failure of the usual rain thus deprives the labouring class, as a whole, not only of the ordinary supplies of food obtainable at prices within their reach, but also of the sole employment by which they can earn the means of procuring [obtaining] it. The complete remedy for this condition of things will be found only in the development of industries other than agriculture and independent of the fluctuations [extreme changes] of the seasons.

13. *Jawaharlal Nehru, commenting on India's population in the first half of the 20th century*

Excessive population is unfortunate and steps should be taken to curb it wherever necessary; but the density of India still compares favourably with that of many industrialised countries. It is only excessive for a predominantly agricultural community, and under a proper economic system the entire population can be made productive and should add to the wealth of the country. As a matter of fact, great density of population exists only in special areas, like Bengal and the Gangetic valley, and vast areas are still sparsely populated. It is worth remembering that Great Britain is more than twice as densely populated as India.

NOTE: (a) India's population rose from 177.9 million in 1851, to 283.9 million in 1901, to 389 million in 1941; (b) India was hit by a number of severe famines at the end of the 19th century. The famine of 1896–97 affected nearly 97 million people over an area of 505,000 square miles and claimed over 5 million lives. The famine of 1899 affected 59 million people over an area of 475,000 square miles and claimed 2 million lives. Famines became less frequent in the 20th century but they were never completely eradicated. The Bengal famine of 1943 affected 60 million people over an area of 77,000 square miles and claimed $1\frac{1}{2}$ million lives.

THE HOME CHARGES

14. *The views of Rajat K Ray, an Indian historian*

India obtained for these charges a well-organised framework of defence and law and order, but it was undoubtedly a very expensive system and many of the charges were for military operations outside India in defence of British imperial (not Indian national) interests. Much more productive in a visible manner was the railway and irrigation network financed by British loans – loans of a size which could not have been raised in India in the nineteenth century. Nevertheless these were 'guaranteed' loans, which ensured private profit at public risk ... The stores purchased in Britain for the construction projects of the public works department – rolling stock, locomotives, various engineering materials – represented, of course, a definite value to India, but the growth of the engineering industries in India was inhibited by the systematic purchase of these stores in Britain. Thus, the indirect benefits of railway and canal construction, i.e. the stimulus to heavy industry, took place more in Britain than in India.

15. PERCENTAGE BREAKDOWN OF GOVERNMENT OF INDIA SPENDING

Year	Administration	Debt Services	Defence	Education	Medical & Public Health	Capital Works	Others
1913–14	27	2	25	4	2	18	23
1917–18	27	8	33	4	2	5	21
1921–22	24	8	33	4	2	12	18
1931–32	28	12	28	7	3	5	20
1946–47	15	6	26	3	2	26	22

NOTE: Capital works included spending on railways, buildings, roads and irrigation. Between 1898 and 1939, railways accounted for 45 per cent of spending on Capital Works, roads and buildings for 36 per cent, and irrigation for 12 per cent.

THE BURDEN OF EMPIRE

16. *Views of Mr T R Buchanan, a British MP and a member of the Royal Commission on Expenditure in India which reported in 1900*

India's financial relations to the Government of the United Kingdom differ fundamentally from those of the Colonies or any other part of the Empire.

Not only are all home civil charges for the Colonies and dependencies borne by the Home Government, but large grants (amounting to several hundred thousand pounds annually) in aid of the administration and development of many colonies and dependencies are made from the Imperial Exchequer.

No colony or dependency makes any contribution towards the diplomatic or consular service of the Empire ...

The position of India is very different. She pays the whole cost of the India Office and its staff, and the office itself was built and is maintained out of Indian funds. She pays a considerable proportion of the charge for missions and consulates in Persia, and China, and other places, and in defraying [paying] the expenses of the government of Aden – a fortress a thousand miles from her shores – she discharges duties and bears expenses, elsewhere looked upon as exclusively Imperial ...

In so far as the military defence of India is concerned, India pays everything, the United Kingdom nothing.

India bears the entire cost of the army, British and Native [Indian], within her borders, the entire cost of the transport of British troops both to and from India ...

It should be noted that she not merely pays and maintains the British troops within her borders, but provides guns, ammunition, and warlike stores for them, and builds and maintains all barracks ...

India has also been called upon from time to time to lend her troops for military service outside her own frontiers and to pay a part, and sometimes the whole, of the expenses of these non-Indian wars.

It cannot be a matter of surprise that those responsible for the Government of India have frequently protested against this apparently unjust treatment, and that ground has been afforded for the expression of a sense of injustice on the part of the Indian taxpayer.

NOTE: Between 1858 and 1914, Indian troops served on a large scale in the second Afghan War (1878–1880) and the third Burmese War (1885), and on a smaller scale at Perak in Malaysia (1875), in Egypt (1882), in the Sudan (1885 and 1896), during the Boer War in South Africa (1899–1902) and during the Boxer Rebellion in China (1900–1901).

INDUSTRIAL DEVELOPMENT IN INDIA

17. The views of M E Chamberlain, a British historian

Finally, it must be said that Indian industries had begun to develop before World War 1 whether because of, or in spite of, the British presence. Some, although not all, of the capital came from Britain. Bengal became an area of jute manufacture as well as producing raw jute. The first Indian jute-spinning mill was established near Serampore in 1855 by two Scots and an Indian. The first power loom began to operate in 1859.

Dundee protested but to no avail and by 1908 the Indian production surpassed that of Dundee. The Indian group most active in establishing new industries were the Parsis of Bombay. One such man, Cawasji Daver, established a cotton-spinning factory at Bombay in 1854. Indian cotton manufacture boomed during the American Civil War. By 1914 India was the fourth greatest cotton-manufacturing nation in the world and Sir Percival Griffiths draws attention to the fact that Lancashire provided the machinery and a great part of the technical know-how. If Lancashire wished to repress the Indian industry it spoke with a divided voice. In 1907 another Parsi family, the Tatas, founded the great Tata iron and steel works and insisted that the capital should come from Indian sources. It developed into the largest such works in the British Empire and India became sixth among the steel-producing nations of the world. Other industries too were developing, paper, brick, hardware, soap and cement among them. Hydro-electric works were established in the Mysore gold fields in 1903 and just before World War 1 the Tata family were completing a project to supply hydro-electric power to Bombay. In 1914 India was certainly not an industrial desert, kept as an area of primary production [a supplier of raw materials] for the British manufacturer.

18. Percentage distribution of the Indian workforce

	1901	1911	1921	1931	1951
Agriculture	73.2	74.8	76.1	75.2	75.7
Industry	1i.2	11.0	10.0	9.8	10.4
Trade and Commerce	5.1	5.4	5.7	5.6	1.5
Transport and Communications	1.1	1.2	1.0	1.1	1.5
Other Services	9.3	7.6	7.2	8.2	7.2

19. The views of Neil Charlesworth, a British historian

In fact British India's heavy industrial development was not as rudimentary [backward] as is sometimes assumed. Coal production, mainly based on the Raniganj and Jharia fields in the Bengal Presidency, began to expand rapidly in the late nineteenth and early twentieth centuries as demand from the railways was increasingly channelled towards Indian coal. By 1914 total coal production exceeded fifteen million tons per annum and India had become a net exporter of coal ... Nevertheless, the limitations of modern industrialisation in the nineteenth century also need great emphasis. India entirely lacked the major 'new' industries, such as chemicals and heavy electricals, which in

Europe seemed vital to successful rapid industrial development after 1870. Modern industry, too, remained a very thinly spread phenomenon; the industrial census of 1911 recorded only just over 7000 units throughout British India employing more than twenty workers and more than a third of these did not use mechanical power.

20. Sir Penderel Moon, a British civil servant in India (1929–44) speaking after independence about what he saw as the major economic question in India

How could the standard of living be raised in this vast land of peasants? I travelled through Russia on my way home on leave in 1937 to see if I could gain any guidance from the USSR. I wanted to give a broadcast talk on it on my return to Lahore but was not allowed to do so. But I felt that a foreign power could not achieve the revolutionary steps that would be necessary to change Indian peasant life. Then I asked myself, 'Should one really try to change it.' I can't answer that question. But obviously the Indian intelligentsia [educated classes] wanted to change it and I felt that the British Raj [Government] would have to give way to an Indian Raj if any change was to be affected [introduced].

21. The views of Rajat K Ray, an Indian historian

Let there be no lack of clarity about this. Only savage, single-minded determination and will-power, that brooked [tolerated] no obstacle or resistance, that did not quail [lose courage] at any sight of privation [hardship] or suffering, could have carried the Indian economy forward at a pace comparable to that of Japan or Russia during the inter-war period. Such a procedure needed, above all, an aggressive appetite for transformation [a strong desire for change], that had characterised Japanese and Russian society from the late ninetenth century.

CHAPTER SIX

THE GROWTH OF NATIONALISM

The importance of Western education

Of all the influences which the British introduced into India, Western education was perhaps the most important. The growth of education was very uneven. It was more visible in Bengal, Bombay and Madras. These were the areas which had been longest exposed to British influence. More money was spent on higher education. Little progress was made in providing education for women. Generally speaking, Muslims were slower in adapting to the new education than Hindus. However, in the second half of the nineteenth century, a new class of Western-educated Indians began to emerge. Their numbers were inevitably small. By the beginning of the twentieth century there were about 30,000 Indian graduates, roughly 1 to every 10,000 of the total population.

The growth of education had two important results. First, it enabled a number of Indians to respond to the challenge of Western ideas, particularly about religion. Christian missionaries painted a negative picture of Hinduism. They said it was a pagan religion, based on superstitious beliefs and barbaric customs. A steady stream of learned Hindus answered these criticisms by reviving the greatness of ancient India. Their work was made that much easier when a number of European scholars produced translations of the ancient Hindu religious epics and scriptures. Sanskrit, the language of ancient India, was shown to be the equal of, and probably superior to, Latin and Greek. Many Hindus took a new pride in their own culture, history and religion. They became involved in movements to defend Hinduism against the attacks of Christian missionaries. The second result of the growth of education was that the Indians who benefited became more familiar with Western ideas about representative or parliamentary government. They began to argue that Indians should be given greater political opportunities in the government of their own country.

Rammohan Roy and Swami Vivekanada

At opposite ends of the nineteenth century, Rammohan Roy and Swami Vivekananda were good examples of the first process. Rammohan Roy (1772–1833) was a Hindu social and religious reformer from Bengal. He was fluent in Bengali, Sanskrit, Arabic and English. One of the first Indians to establish newspapers, he also started a number of secondary schools, led a successful campaign against *sati* and founded a religious society, the Brahmo Samaj (Society of God). Roy welcomed Western influences if he thought India would benefit. But he also attacked Christian missionaries who insulted Hinduism. In defending Hinduism, Roy argued that the West owed much to Asia (Nos 1–2). At the end of the nineteenth century, Swami Vivekananda (1863–1902) acted as India's missionary to the West by preaching the greatness of Hinduism. In 1893 he addressed the First World Parliament of Religions at Chicago. In his writings and speeches, Vivekananda defended image-worship (No 3), attacked those of his own countrymen who copied Western ways (No 4) and argued that India had a mission of its own to conquer the world (No 5). Vivekananda was an important influence on some of the ideas later developed by Gandhi.

Of course the great mass of the Hindu population of India remained unaffected by the ideas of men such as Rammohan Roy and Vivekananda. Equally, Hindu society remained divided. Some Hindus joined social reform movements and campaigned against other practices – child marriage and the treatment of widows – which they regarded as unjust. Others, the more conservative, joined movements to defend traditional beliefs and practices. But the revival of Hinduism had at least exploded the myth of Western superiority (No 6).

The demands of Western-educated Indians

Western-educated Indians became lawyers, journalists, teachers and doctors. However, the career which carried most prestige – as a government civil servant in the Indian Civil Service (ICS) – was largely closed to them. The regulations which governed entry into the ICS made it very difficult for Indians to become members. Entry was by means of a competitive examination which was held only in England. It was expensive for Indian candidates to travel to Britain to sit the examination and they were also given little time in which to prepare. In 1876 the upper age limit for the examination was fixed at nineteen. Educated Indians campaigned for the age limit to be raised and for a simultaneous entrance examination to be held in India. They held meetings in India, presented petitions to the government and wrote letters to the press. They also sent deputations to Britain in an attempt to influence Parliament in London. But the British Government would not be persuaded. By 1900, of the 1142 members of the ICS, only 60 were Indians.

During the second half of the nineteenth century, the growing numbers of Western-educated Indians could be seen as the products of the educational system which the British had introduced into India in the 1830s (see chapter 3). These Indians admired Western political ideas and the British system of government. They wanted reforms which would enable Indians to play a greater role in the government of their own country (No 7). As well as the reform of the methods of entry into the ICS, they wanted to see Indians appointed to the Viceroy's Council or Cabinet. They also wanted to see Indians represented in greater numbers on the legislative councils. Each province of India had its own legislative council and there was also an Imperial legislative council for the whole of India. The majority of council members were not elected. Instead they were nominated by the government. The councils had no power. They could discuss new laws but they could not change government policy.

The Indian National Congress 1885

In order to press their demands for reforms, Western-educated Indians formed political organisations in their own provinces. Their activities convinced some of the leaders that they needed a national organisation for the whole of India. In December 1885 the first meeting of an Indian National Congress was held at Bombay. The early Congress has usually been described as a middle-class movement, dominated by lawyers. A high proportion of members came from the professions but after lawyers, landlords were the largest single group (No 8).

The leaders of the early Congress were anxious to point out that they were not disloyal. They were moderates and they did not demand the end of British rule (No 9). They criticised the expense of British administration in India and certain aspects of British economic policy (fig 6.1). But in other ways they saw British influence as constructive. Western education, Western law and Western technology were giving India a sense of national unity. Railways were next in importance to education. Educated Indians discovered more about their own country simply because they were able to travel greater distances in much shorter time.

The early Congress was moderate in its methods as well as its goals. It relied on speeches, petitions and deputations to promote its aims. It was not a political party in the modern sense. Between annual sessions – it met for a few days in December each year – it

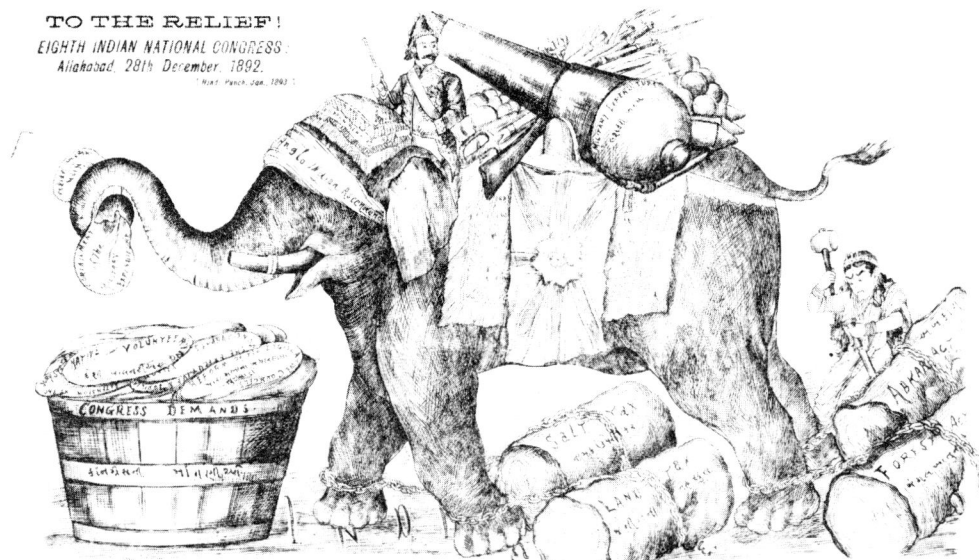

6.1 *A cartoon from Hindi Punch, January 1893. The elephant represents India, weighed down by the burden of military expenditure and various taxes which are chained to its feet. The figure to the right represents the Indian National Congress attempting to break free of some of the taxes. The barrel to the left contains some of the Congress demands. The elephant eats from the barrel despite the fact that it is blindfolded by the 'Anglo-Indian Ascendancy' which represents the strength of British interests in India.*

was hardly visible in India. It had no permanent source of finance and relied on donations from princes and businessmen. Most of what little money it had was spent on a British Committee of Congress which was established in London. In the early years Congress was as much concerned to influence public opinion in Britain as it was to put pressure on the British Government in India. In 1892 Dadabhai Naoroji, one of the moderate Congress leaders, became the first Indian MP in Britain.

White Racism

The growth of nationalism in India was also encouraged by white racism. Carriages and compartments on railways and steamers were reserved for whites only. Educated Indians faced discrimination in their search for jobs. Labourers on tea plantations were physically abused and beaten. British soldiers were often guilty of racial attacks (No 10). The most famous case of racism was that of the Ilbert Bill in 1883. Taking its name from the law member of the Viceroy's Council, the Ilbert Bill was designed to give Indian magistrates the power to try Europeans living in country districts for criminal offences. Indian magistrates already possessed this power in the towns. The Bill raised a storm of protest from the Eurpean planters and settlers, particularly in Bengal. They organised themselves in a European and Anglo-Indian Defence Association to fight the Bill (No 11). The Government of India was forced to give in to their pressure and the Bill was watered down. Europeans were given the right to claim that at least half the jury should be European if they were brought to court. The agitation against the Ilbert Bill served as a lesson to those Indians who wanted to press claims of their own. It was no coincidence that the Indian National Congress was established two years later.

British responses to the early Indian National Congress

But the early Congress made little headway. Many British officials did not think that Western-educated Indians were fit for government service. They referred to them as *babus*. A term of respect in Bengali and Hindi, *babu* was used by the British in an insulting way to describe those educated Indians, particularly Bengalis, who wanted reforms (No 12). The British argued that Congress was unrepresentative of the Indian people as a whole and paid little attention to its demands (Nos 13–14).

The Extremist alternative

The failure of the moderates led, at the turn of the century, to the growth of a more radical, extremist faction within Congress. The extremists did not share the moderates' view about the constructive role of British influence in India. They were not prepared to wait for the British to grant reforms as if they were handing out rewards for good behaviour (No 15). The extremists organised festivals to revive patriotic traditions and set up schools which encouraged physical sports (No 16). They also called for a boycott of British goods (No 17). A boycott movement gathered strength as a result of a decision by the Viceroy, Lord Curzon, to partition the province of Bengal in 1905 (fig 6.2). The British claimed that partition was necessary because Bengal was too big to be governed as a single province. But partition was seen by the educated Hindus of Bengal as a deliberate move to weaken Bengali nationalism (the province was in fact reunited in 1911). The boycott

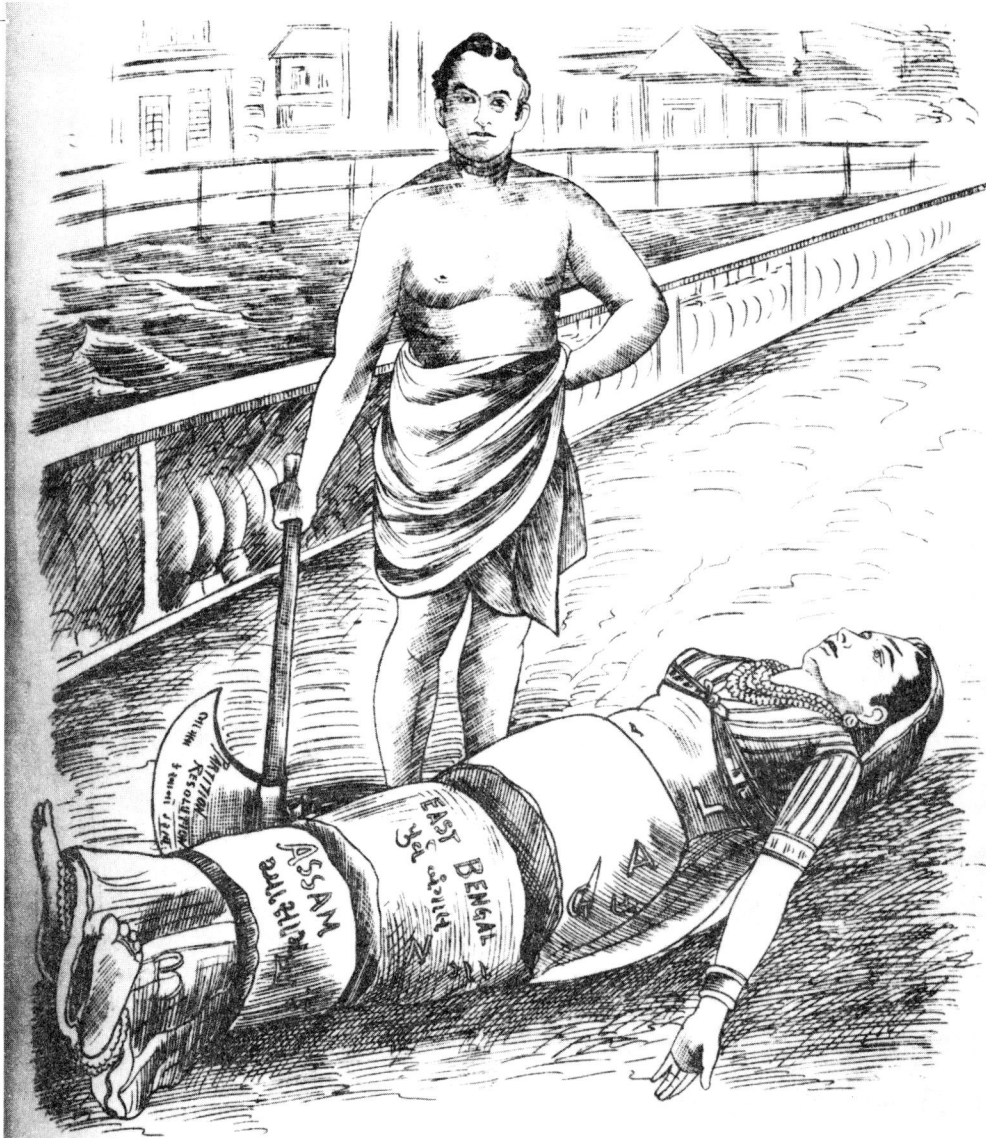

VANDALISM!
OR, THE PARTITION OF BENGAL!

[A resolution on the partition of Bengal has been published. Bengal will be divided and a new province will be created which will be entitled Eastern Bengal and Assam. Well may the Bengal papers go into mourning.]

6.2 The Partition of Bengal: a cartoon from Hindi Punch, July 1905. Lord Curzon, the Viceroy, is the figure with the axe.

movement was strongest in Bengal itself. The boycott of British goods went hand-in-hand with the *swadeshi* movement. Meaning 'of one's own country', the *swadeshi* movement was designed to encourage self-help through the production of home-made goods (No 18).

The Russo–Japanese War and Indian Literature

Indian nationalists were also encouraged by Japan's defeat of Tsarist Russia in the war of 1904–5. This was the first time in modern history that an Asian country had defeated a European power (No 19). Indian literature provided further inspiration. The novel *Anandamath* by Bankimchandra Chatterjee told of a band of holy men attempting to free Bengal from Muslim rule in the eighteenth century. The novel contained a hymn, *Bande Mataram* (Hail to thee, O Mother), which became a national slogan and a national song. During the agitation against the partition of Bengal, the British government issued an order making it illegal to shout 'Bande Mataram' in the streets (Nos 20–21).

The Indian terrorist movement

Some extremists went beyond the method of boycott. They resorted to revolutionary violence and terrorism. Bengal in particular was the scene of a number of bombings and assassinations (No 22). Abroad, in places such as London and Paris, Indian students organised themselves into revolutionary cells. They included V D Savarkar, author of *The Indian War of Independence of 1857* (see chapter 4, No 14). Faced by the growth of violence, the British Government tried to split the moderate nationalists from the extremists. To gain the support of the moderates, the British introduced some modest reforms in the 1909 Indian Councils Act. An Indian was appointed to the Viceroy's Council and more Indians were elected to the legislative councils. But the British also responded to the violence with a series of repressive measures. The press was tightly controlled. The main extremist leaders were arrested and deported. Meanwhile, within the Indian National Congress, the debate over tactics produced a damaging split between moderates and extremists in 1907. Congress had established itself as a political force but British rule in India still seemed as strong as ever. Equally, the campaign against the partition of Bengal demonstrated that nationalism in India was not as yet a mass movement. The campaign was led by the educated classes, it was very much a Hindu movement and it was not supported by the Muslims. The significance of this last point is examined in Chapter 9.

THE REVIVAL OF HINDUISM

1. Rammohan Roy attacks missionaries (1823)

But during the last twenty years, a body of English Gentlemen who are called missionaries have been publicly endeavouring, in several ways, to convert Hindoos and Mussulmans of this country into Christianity. The first way is of publishing and distributing among the natives various books, large and small, reviling both religions, and abusing and ridiculing the gods and saints of the former; the second way is that of standing in front of the doors of the natives or in the public roads to preach the excellency of that of others; the third way is that if any natives of low origin become Christian from the desire of gain or from any other motives, these Gentlemen employ and maintain them as a necessary encouragement to others to follow their example.

2. Rammohan Roy defends Hindu culture and religion (1823)

If by the 'ray of intelligence' for which the Christian says we are indebted to the English, he means the introduction of useful mechanical arts, I am ready to express my assent and also my gratitude; but with respect to *science, literature or religion,* I do not acknowledge that we are placed under any obligation. For by a reference to History it may be proved that the world was indebted to *our* ancestors for the first dawn of knowledge, which sprang up in the East, and thanks to the Goddess of Wisdom, we have ... a language of our own which distinguishes us from other nations who cannot express scientific or abstract ideas without borrowing the language of foreigners.

Before 'A Christian' indulged in a tirade [verbal abuse] about persons being degraded by '*Asiatic* effeminacy' he should have recollected that almost all the ancient prophets ... venerated by Christians, nay even Jesus Christ himself ... were Asiatics. So that if a Christian thinks it degrading to be born or to reside in Asia, he directly reflects upon them ...

3. Swami Vivekananda defends image-worship (1901)

Those reformers who preach against image-worship, or what they describe as idolatory – to them I say: 'Brothers! If you are fit to worship God-without-Form discarding any external help, do so, but why do you condemn others who cannot do the same?'

4. Swami Vivekananda condemns the 'foolishness' of imitating the West (1899)

O India, this is your terrible danger. The spell of imitating the West is getting such a strong hold upon you, that what is good or what is bad is no longer decided by reason

[or] judgement ... Whatever ideas, whatever manners the white men praise or like, are good; whatever things they dislike or censure [condemn] are bad! Alas! What can be a more tangible [evident] proof of foolishness than this? The Western ladies move freely everywhere – therefore, that is good; they chose for themselves their husbands – therefore, that is the highest step of advancement; the Westerners disapprove of our dress, decorations, food, and ways of living – therefore, they must be very bad; the Westerners condemn image-worship as sinful – surely then, image-worship is the greatest sin, there is no doubt of it! ... We are not discussing here whether these customs deserve countenance [approval] or rejection; but if the mere disapproval of the Westerners be the measure of the abominableness of our manners and customs, then it is our duty to raise our emphatic protest against it.

5. *Swami Vivekananda on India's mission to conquer the world (1897)*

This is the great ideal before us, and every one must be ready for it – the conquest of the whole world by India – nothing less than that ... Let foreigners come and flood the land with their armies, never mind. Up, India and conquer the world with your spirituality! Aye, as has been declared on this soil first, love must conquer hatred, hatred cannot conquer itself. Materialism and all its miseries can never be conquered by materialism. Armies when they attempt to conquer armies only multiply and make brutes of humanity. Spirituality must conquer the West ... The world wants it; without it the world will be destroyed. The whole of the Western world is on a volcano which may burst tomorrow, go to pieces tomorrow. They have searched every corner of the world and have found no respite [peace] ... Now is the time to work so that India's spirituality may penetrate deep into the West ... There is no other alternative, we must do it or die. The only condition of national life, of awakened and vigorous national life, is the conquest of the world by Indian thought.

6. *Surendranath Banerjea, one of the founders of the Indian National Congress, in a speech to the Oxford Union (a debating society at Oxford University) in 1890*

The statement has been made in the course of this debate that the Indians before the advent [arrival] of the English were a pack of barbarians or semi-barbarians; I believe that was the language used. Let me remind this house that they come – the Hindus of India, the race to which I have the honour to belong – (loud cheers) – they come from a great and ancient stock; that at a time when the ancestors of the most enlightened European nations were roaming in their native woods and forests, our fathers had founded great empires, established noble cities, and cultivated a system of ethics [moral standards], a system of religion, and a noble language which at the present moment excites the admiration of the civilized world. (Loud cheers).

THE EARLY INDIAN NATIONAL CONGRESS

7. *Lal Mohan Ghose, an Indian lawyer, speaking at Bombay in 1880, five years before the first meeting of the Indian National Congress*

You [the British] have for a long time past given us the blessings of a liberal education. Our minds are expanded under the generous influence of Western culture. We are deeply grateful to you for all these benefits. But remember, as our intellectual faculties are developed, so are our aspirations, both personal and national, sharpened and stimulated ... Remember that the study of European history, and particularly of the history of England and of English political institutions, is not calculated to deaden, but on the contrary to rouse and fire those instincts of patriotism, which have slumbered in the national breast of India for many centuries. Open up a career for those whom you yourselves have fitted for a high and useful career, and remember, above all, that the surest way to make the people of this country disloyal and to array them in bitter opposition to the British government, is to close and shut up every avenue for ... their ambition and aspirations.

8. *Congress delegates 1892–1909*

Year	Place	Total no. of delegates	Lawyers	Landed Classes	Commercial Classes	Journalists and newspapermen	Medical profession	Teachers
1892	Allahabad	625	237	161	70	39	22	21
1893	Lahore	867	305	134	152	51	22	28
1894	Madras	1163	544	211	158	36	12	61
1895	Poona	1584	457	149	437	26	38	50
1896	Calcutta	784	312	224	88	23	58	32
1897	Amraoti	692	135	257	160	20	8	16
1898	Madras	614	259	102	65	23	12	40
1899	Lucknow	739	176	112	100	21	17	18
1900	Lahore	567	245	32	77	23	23	20
1901	Calcutta	896	370	241	73	39	33	32
1902	Ahmedabad	471	168	162	23	12	13	4
1903	Madras	538	295	92	52	15	13	11
1904	Bombay	1010	362	110	219	27	34	12
1905	Banares	757	372	134	100	9	35	26
1906	Calcutta	1663	705	394	230	50	53	50
1908	Madras	626	369	95	60	17	11	12
1909	Lahore	243	131	19	27	10	4	5
Total		13,839	5,442	2,629	2,091	441	408	438

9. *Dadabhai Naoroji's presidential address at the second meeting of the Indian National Congress, Calcutta, 1886*

It is our good fortune that we are under a rule which makes it possible for us to meet in this manner. (Cheers). It is under the civilizing rule of the Queen and people of England that we meet here together, hindered by none, and are freely allowed to speak our minds without the least fear and without the least hesitation. Such a thing is possible under British rule and British rule only. (Loud cheers). Then I put the question plainly: Is this Congress a nursery for sedition and rebellion against the British Government (cries of 'no, no'); or, is it another stone in the foundation of the stability of that Government? (Cries of 'yes, yes'.)

WHITE RACISM

10. *Mr Dinshaw Edulji Wacha to Dadabhai Naoroji, 3 October 1891*

You will read in the papers that our last Criminal Sessions [sitting of a criminal court] was a Session of disagreeable surprises. European murderers of Natives are daily on the increase. Soldiers chiefly are the brutal offenders. With or without provocation they wildly shoot poor Natives, helpless villagers and so on. And when they are brought to the bar of justice they are always acquitted on some plea or other. The Ahmednagar murder case tried last Sessions was a scandal. Even the English dailies [newspapers] for very shame are obliged to confess that there has been a miscarrige of justice – the circumstantial evidence was so overwhelming.

NOTE: The Ahmednagar murder case referred to two British sergeants who were arrested on suspicion of having killed an Indian, put on trial, but then set free for want of evidence.

11. *W S Blunt recording in his diary the views of Sir Alfred Lyall, Governor of the North-Western Provinces, about the Ilbert Bill, 10 January 1884*

Talking of the Ilbert Bill, he said it was, as far as the Anglo-Indians were concerned, a local Bengal measure. It was quite true [that] the Assam planters regarded it as an attempt to do away with their right of beating niggers.

Note to Table 8: The 1907 meeting at Surat was the scene of a violent clash between moderates and extremists and the meeting broke up on the first day.

THE BRITISH RESPONSE TO THE DEMANDS OF WESTERN-EDUCATED INDIANS AND THE INDIAN NATIONAL CONGRESS

12. *The views of Lord Lytton, Viceroy 1876–1880*

[T]he Baboodom of lower Bengal, though disloyal, is fortunately cowardly and its only revolver is its ink bottle; which though dirty, is not dangerous ... It is one thing to admit the public into your park, and quite another thing to admit it into your drawing room ... Already great mischief has been done by the deplorable tendency of second-rate Indian officials and superficial English philanthropists to ignore the essential and insurmountable distinctions of race qualities, which are fundamental to our position in India; and thus, unintentionally, to pamper the conceit and vanity of half-educated natives, to the serious detriment [harm] of commonsense, and of the wholesome recognition of realities.

NOTE: A philanthropist is someone who works for the well-being of other people. A handful of British civil servants in India were in fact sympathetic to the demands being made by Western-educated Indians. Allan Octavian Hume, a retired Indian Civil Servant, played a leading role in the establishment of the Indian National Congress in 1885.

13. *The views of Lord Dufferin, Viceroy 1884–1888*

Consequently it must be admitted that, out of a population of two hundred millions, there are only a very few thousands who may be considered to possess adequate qualifications for taking an intelligent view of ... local public affairs ... while those who may be credited with capacity for comprehending ... the larger problems which are being presented from day to day to the consideration of the Government would have to be counted rather by tens than by hundreds. To extend, therefore, to this infinitesimal [tiny] and only partially qualified fraction of the people of India anything beyond consultative, critical and suggestive powers ... would be evidently impracticable. The chief concern of the Government of India is to protect and foster the interests of the people of India, and the people of India are not the seven or eight thousand students who have graduated at the Universities, or the Pleaders [lawyers] recruited from their numbers who are practising at the Courts of Justice, or the newspaper writers, or the Europeanized Zemindars [landlords], or the wealthy traders, but the voiceless millions whom neither education, nor civilization, nor the influence of European ideas or modern thought, have in the slightest degree ... transformed [changed] from what their forefathers were a thousand years ago.

14. The views of Lord Curzon, Viceroy 1899–1905

My own belief is that the [Indian National] Congress is tottering to its fall, and one of my greatest ambitions while in India is to assist it to a peaceful demise ... the composition of Congress, at any rate in recent years, [has] deprived them of any right to pose as the representative of more than a small section of the community.

THE EXTREMIST ALTERNATIVE

15. Bal Gangadhar Tilak, a leading extremist, attacking Dadabhai Naoroji and Gopal Krishna Gokhale, two moderate members of the Indian National Congress, January 1907

[T]he venerable leader [Dadabhai Naoroji] who presided over the recent Congress was the first to tell us that the drain [of wealth] from the country was ruining it, and if the drain was to continue, there was some great disaster awaiting us. So terribly convinced was he of this that he went over from here to England and spent twenty-five years of his life trying to convince the English people of the injustice that is being done to us. He worked very hard. He had conversations and interviews with Secretaries of State, with Members of Parliament – and with what result? He has come here at the age of eighty-two to tell us that he is bitterly disappointed. Mr Gokhale, I know, is not disappointed. He is a friend of mine and I believe that this is his honest conviction. Mr Gokhale is not disappointed but is prepared to wait another eighty years till he is disappointed like Mr Dadabhai.

16. Article by Tilak in his Marathi newspaper, Kesari, describing the annual Shivaji festival, 15 June 1897. Shivaji was a seventeenth century Maratha warrior who led a major revolt against the Mughal empire

The Shri Shivaji coronation festival ... was brought to a close last night. The temple of the god Vithal ... was decorated in excellent style for the festival. An image of Shri Shivaji on horseback was installed and around it were arranged pictures of Shri Shivaji Maharaja drawn by different artists ... Professor Jiniswale said on this occasion that the reason why Shri Shivaji Maharaja should be considered superior to Caesar and Napoleon was that, while the great men of Europe were actuated [motivated] by ambition alone ... the uncommon attributes [qualities] displayed by our Maharaja were not the blaze of the fire of ambition ... but were the outcome of the terrible irritation at the ruin of his country and religion by foreigners.

On the morning of the second day there were athletic sports ... The students of the New English School and the New Marathi School acquitted [conducted] themselves creditably in their performance ... We hope that the students of other schools will follow their example in this matter. The students attending the various schools as well as the people attending the gymnasia at this place will not find a better occasion than the festival of the anniversary of Shivaji's birth for exhibiting their skill in manly sports.

17. *Tilak on the meaning of boycott, 2 January 1907*

We are not armed, and there is no necessity for arms either. We have a stronger weapon, a political weapon, in boycott. We have perceived [noticed] one fact, that the whole of this administration, which is carried on by a handful of Englishmen, is carried on with our assistance. We are all in subordinate service. This whole government is carried on with our assistance and they try to keep us in ignorance of our power of cooperation between ourselves ... The point is to have the entire control in our hands. I want to have the key of my house, and not merely one stranger turned out of it. Self-government is our goal; we want a control over our administrative machinery. We don't want to become clerks and remain clerks ... This is boycott and this is what is meant when we say boycott is a political weapon. We shall not give them assistance to collect revenue and keep peace. We shall not assist them in fighting beyond the frontiers or outside India with Indian blood and money. We shall not assist them in carrying on the administration of justice. We shall have our own courts, and when the time comes we shall not pay taxes. Can you do that by your united efforts? If you can, you are free from tomorrow.

18. *Surendranath Banerjea describing the swadeshi movement in 1905*

[T]he *Swadeshi* movement made steady headway. Throughout, the dominating idea was to be independent of Manchester and of the foreign market for our ordinary wearing apparel [clothes], our *dhoties* [waistcloths for men] and *sarees* [dresses for women]. Bombay was partly supplying them; and the Bombay cotton mills had a highly prosperous time during the height of the *Swadeshi* movement. But it was felt that Bengal might, to some extent, supply her own needs. There was a cotton mill at Serampore on the [river] Hughli, which had been in existence for some time. It was resolved to buy up this mill and to extend its operations ... An appeal was issued. I was one of the signatories. The money was easily found, being largely subscibed by our middle class people and even by our women-folk. The mill was purchased, extended and re-named. It was called the 'Banga Luxmi Mill', as a compliment to the gentler sex, who had shown a practical interest in the concern.

19. Jawaharlal Nehru writing in his Autobiography about the Russo–Japanese War

The next important event that I remember affecting me was the Russo–Japanese War. Japanese victories stirred up my imagination and I waited eagerly for the papers for fresh news daily. I invested in a large number of books on Japan and tried to read some of them ... Nationalistic ideas filled my mind. I mused [wondered] of Indian freedom and Asiatic freedom from the thraldom [captivity] of Europe. I dreamt of brave deeds, of how, sword in hand, I would fight for India and help in freeing her. I was fourteen.

20. A British view of 'Bande Mataram', by James Campbell Kerr, Personal Assistant to the Director of Criminal Intelligence in India, 1907–13

The greeting 'Bande Mataram' became the war-cry of the extremist party in Bengal; it was raised at political meetings to welcome popular leaders and to express approval of particularly exciting passages in their speeches, and also occasionally as a shout of defiance in the streets. The *Bande Mataram* song was also very frequently sung at political gatherings. It was of course invariably represented by the Bengali nationalist press that the cry of 'Bande Mataram', as it meant nothing more than 'Hail! Mother', must be perfectly harmless; but although the words are harmless enough they were used as an outward sign of sympathy with revolution and defiance of Government.

21. An Indian view of 'Bande Mataram', by Surendranath Banerjea

The *Bande Mataram* circular ... was issued by the new Government of East Bengal, and it declared the shouting of *Bande Mataram* in the public streets to be illegal; and an authority in the person of a high European official, supposed to be versed [informed] in the ancient lore [traditional belief] of our country, was found, who went so far as to assert that it was an invocation [calling upon] to the goddess Kali [Hindu goddess of destruction] for vengeance. Where he got this idea from is difficult to know. The opening lines of the *Bande Mataram* are the words of a song, full of love for, and devotion to, the motherland ... 'I salute the mother, the mother of us all, namely the motherland' – that is the plain meaning of the words. But amid the excitement which prevailed in official circles a sinister meaning was read into this very innocent formula, and a circular was issued by the Government suppressing the cry in the streets.

22. The terrorist movement. Extract from the diary of James Dunlop Smith, Private Secretary to the Viceroy, Lord Minto (1905–10), 5 May 1908

Mr Kingsford, ICS, the Chief Presidency Magistrate in Calcutta, had had to dispose of several sedition cases. He had had such a hard time for over a year that he was transferred to Muzaffarpur in Tirhoot. The police heard that some men had left Calcutta to assassinate him, and a few evenings ago two Bengali youths threw a bomb into a carriage in which Mrs and Miss Kennedy were driving home from the Club in the dark. Both were frightfully injured and died. Mr Kingsford's carriage was not far behind. Both men were eventually arrested and one committed suicide when he was caught. The other made a full confession with the result that the police made an organised raid on certain houses in Calcutta.

The searchers found a well-equipped bomb factory with dry batteries, bottles of nitric acid, stocks of gunpowder, dynamite, cartridges and detonators, iron casing for shells, moulds, thermometers, test tubes, glass bulbs, and all the paraphernalia of such dens, carefully packed and stored on the floor, and low shelves were completely loaded with bombs, dynamite cartridges and ammunition for Express, Martini-Henry and revolver. Some of the stuff was in steel trunks, and in turning out one of these the searchers found beneath some bombs a picture from a London Illustrated Magazine showing the attempted assassination of the King and Queen of Spain on their wedding day, and on the back of this a sketch of the bomb used on the occasion. Inside a bomb-shell was a mass of correspondence ... of a most startling and illuminating nature ... It affords ample evidence that this conspiracy of Anarchists is not a thing of very recent growth, but has been nursed for some time. It also has substantial financial backing. One of the experts of the gang is a man who was sent some time back to Paris to study the latest developments in the manufacture and use of infernal machines ... The Paris Police warned us long ago about the Bengali centre in Paris.

CHAPTER SEVEN

THE AMRITSAR MASSACRE 1919

The Massacre

On Sunday 13 April 1919, at about 5.15 in the afternoon, Brigadier-General Reginald Edward Harry Dyer arrived at the Jallianwala Bagh, a piece of wasteland near the centre of Amritsar, the second city of the Punjab in Northern India. Dyer was a British officer in the Indian Army. He had with him ninety Indian troops of whom fifty were armed with rifles. The Jallianwala Bagh was rectangular in shape and enclosed on all sides by high walls. The main entrance was a narrow passage through which Dyer marched his men. There were four or five other openings through which people could get in and out, a few at a time. Upon arrival Dyer saw before him a large crowd which he estimated to be about 5,000–6,000 strong but which was later thought to be in the region of 15,000–20,000. The crowd was unarmed. Standing on a platform in the centre of the crowd a man was speaking. He was about sixty yards away from Dyer and his men. They could not hear what he was saying but they could see him gesturing to the crowd with his arms. Dyer positioned his men on either side of a ridge in front of the main entrance. Without warning to the crowd he gave the order to open fire. As the bullets sprayed into it, the terrified crowd fled towards the handful of exits. In the scramble to escape, hundreds were knocked to the ground and trampled under foot. The firing continued for ten minutes before Dyer ordered his men to stop. He then marched his men out the way they had come in. Behind them they left a scene resembling a battlefield. Official estimates reported 379 dead and 1,200 wounded.

The Enquiries

The shooting at the Jallianwala Bagh was at the time, and has remained since, a subject of considerable controversy. To some, Dyer was a brutal murderer who had ordered the massacre of perfectly innocent people. To others, Dyer was a hero who had saved the Punjab from rebellion and further bloodshed on a much larger scale. How and why did the shooting happen and what were its consequences? In October 1919 the Government of India appointed a Committee of Enquiry. The Committee was asked to report on a series of disturbances which had taken place all over the Punjab in 1919 and also in other parts of India. Known as the Hunter Committee after its Chairman, Lord Hunter, the Committee consisted of eight members. Five, including Hunter, were British. The other three were Indian lawyers. The Committee's report was published in May 1920. Unable to arrive at unanimous conclusions, the Committee produced two reports: a Majority Report representing the views of the British, and a Minority Report representing the views of the Indians. A separate enquiry was undertaken by a Committee appointed by the Indian National Congress. The evidence in this chapter is based on the reports of the Hunter and Congress Committees.

The Background: (1) The Punjab in 1919

The Punjab in 1919 was an unsettled province. A bad harvest had produced food shortages. The recent war in Europe had caused many hardships for the people. The Punjab had provided more fighting men for the war than any other part of India. The province was famous for its martial races. But rumours spread that the government had forced men to enlist in the army. It was also said that people had been forced against their will to make contributions to a War Loan to help finance the war effort. The Lieutenant-Governor of the Punjab, Sir Michael O'Dwyer, was extremely unpopular with Indian politicians (fig 7.1). A firm believer in Britain's mission to rule India, O'Dwyer made no secret of his view that Indians were not fit to govern themselves. He regarded Indian politicians who agitated for reforms as a noisy and troublesome minority. He poured scorn on their ideas of self-government (No 1). But O'Dwyer's attitude seemed to conflict with the new aims of British rule in India. Recognising that India had made a major contribution to the war effort (Nos 2–3), the Government in London issued an important statement in 1917. It declared that it was the goal of British policy to introduce, by stages, self-government in India. As a first step in this direction, a Reforms Act was introduced in 1919. Under the Act, Indian politicians were given responsibility for certain aspects of government in the provinces of British India.

The Background: (2) The Rowlatt Act 1919

There was, however, another aspect to British policy in India at the end of the war. Many British officials were worried about the threat of revolution. There had been an attempt at a rebellion in the Punjab in 1915. It was led by Sikhs who had emigrated to North America. At the beginning of the war they returned to the Punjab with German arms and money. The rebellion failed for lack of popular support. The threat of revolution was more imagined than real. But the British thought otherwise. In March 1919 the Government of India introduce a new law. It was known as the Rowlatt Act. Rowlatt was the name of a High Court Judge who headed a Committee to investigate revolutionary influences. The Act gave the police wide powers to decide which offences amounted to conspiracy against the government. It also provided for speedy trials, not by jury but by special tribunals. Suspects were denied the right to be represented by a lawyer and had no right of appeal against a guilty verdict.

The Rowlatt Act aroused widespread opposition throughout India. Popularly known as the 'Black Act', wild rumours circulated about the new powers which had been given to the police. Most Indian politicians regarded the 1915 uprising in the Punjab as an isolated event. To them the Rowlatt Act was not simply a denial of basic human rights. It also made a mockery of the idea that India would one day enjoy self-government. Opposition to the Act was organised by Gandhi who had returned to India from South Africa at the beginning of 1915. Gandhi decided to launch a campaign of civil disobedience. *Hartal*s (strikes and shop closures) were observed in many cities and towns throughout India on 30 March and 6 April 1919. Gandhi appealed for a non-violent campaign but in Delhi on 30 March the police clashed with demonstrators and a number of people were killed.

The Amritsar Riots

In Amritsar, *hartal*s on the selected dates passed off without incident. But the senior British official, Mr Miles Irving, became increasingly worried about the activities of the organisers – two local politicians, Drs Kitchlew and Satyapal. Irving sent a report to the Government of the Punjab. He received instructions in reply to deport the two politicians to another town 100 miles away. The deportations took place on the morning of 10 April 1919. Irving wanted to carry out the deportations under cover of secrecy but his plans misfired when news of them leaked out.

An angry crowd, small at first but increasing by the minute until it numbered several

SIR MICHAEL O'DWYER—I leave Punjab happy and contented.   MR. PUNCH—Wish you had left earlier!

[Sir Michael O'Dwyer has handed over the charge of his office to his successor Sir Edward Maclagan on the 25th May. In his farewell message he expresses his gratitude to the people of the Punjab for their vigorous support of and hearty co-operation with the administration in these critical years and hopes that it will be possible to abolish Martial Law in certain areas almost at once and, if improvement continues, to dispense with it in the rest within the next few weeks. It has been clear that the great mass of people was actively loyal to the King Emperor. He never doubted the Punjab people and on leaving down office his faith in them was greater than ever.]   [*Hindi Punch, June, 1919.*]

7.1 *A cartoon from Hindi Punch, June 1919, demonstrating the Indian nationalist view of Sir Michael O'Dwyer, Lieutenant-Governor of the Punjab at the time of the Amritsar Massacre.*

79

hundred, gathered at the footbridge over the railway which separated the European living quarters in Amritsar from the main city. The crowd demanded the release of the two politicians. Irving arrived on the scene and attempted, unsuccessfully, to persuade the crowd to disperse. As the crowd pressed forward against the hopelessly outnumbered force of armed police, shots were fired and a number of demonstrators killed. The crowd fell back and made its way towards the main city where British businesses were located. Here the crowd was joined by thousands more as news of the shooting spread. The mob then went on the rampage. The Telegraph Exchange was set on fire. At the railway, a European guard was chased, caught and clubbed to death. Three banks were attacked and one was set on fire and looted. Three bank officials, all European, were beaten to death and their bodies burnt in the street with a pile of bank furniture. A hospital was ransacked as the mob tried to find a woman doctor who managed to escape in disguise with the help of her Indian servant. In a narrow side street a missionary, Miss Sherwood, was set upon by a gang of young men, brutally assaulted and left for dead. She was later rescued by a group of Indians. The Town Hall, three sub-post offices, a Christian church and a missionary school were destroyed by fire (No 4). Rioting and violence also occurred at Lahore, the capital of the Punjab, on 10 April and then spread to the surrounding countryside. Here the main main targets were railways and telegraph lines (Nos 5–6). When they came to investigate, the Hunter and Congress Committees had to decide whether these disturbances represented spontaneous riots or the beginning of an organised rebellion (Nos 7–10).

General Dyer's Proclamations

General Dyer was stationed in the Punjab. He was ordered to proceed to Amritsar on 10 April, the day of the mob violence. He arrived at 9 pm the following day. He met first with Irving and a senior police officer. Irving explained what had happened on the 10th and admitted that the situation was beyond the control of the civil authorities. Without consulting his superiors, Dyer decided that the situation demanded the introduction of martial law. On the morning of 12 April he made a tour of the city with some of his men. He was greeted by jeering crowds. Dyer instructed the police to issue a proclamation warning the people of Amritsar against meetings and acts of violence.

Sunday 13 April was a religious festival and also the day of a cattle and horse fair. Both events attracted peasants from the outlying villages into Amritsar. It was also a worrying day for Dyer. Although there had been no further violence in Amritsar since the outbreak on the 10th, reports were coming in all the time of disturbances in neighbouring districts. During the morning of the 13th, Dyer decided to issue another proclamation. It warned that any gathering of four or more people would be regarded as an unlawful assembly and dispersed by force if necessary. Dyer personally supervised the issue of this proclamation. He made a tour of the city stopping at nineteen places. At each place a drum was beaten and the proclamation was read out four or five times in different languages. Leaflets were also distributed but the proclamation was not posted anywhere in the city. Dyer did not cover the entire city. He cut short his tour at midday when the heat became unbearable. He returned to his headquarters. Here he was told that a meeting had been planned that afternoon. It would be held at the Jallianwala Bagh, a popular venue for festivals and fairs as well as meetings (Nos 11–12). At 4 pm Dyer assembled his men and proceeded to the Jallianwala Bagh. In his written report and under cross-examination before the Hunter Committee, Dyer explained why, when he arrived at the Jallianwala Bagh, he gave the order to open fire without warning (Nos 13–14). Eye-witness accounts spoke of the panic and terror during the ten-minute burst of gunfire (No 15).

Martial Law at Amritsar

Martial law remained in operation at Amritsar until 9 June 1919. During this time the people of the city were made to pay for the violence which had taken place on 10 April. All Indians had to salaam (a form of salute, touching the forehead with the hand in the act of bowing) when they passed Europeans. Those who failed to do so or who did it incorrectly were arrested and imprisoned. Sometimes they were flogged. People were arrested and imprisoned for long periods without being charged. There were allegations of police brutality and torture. This picture was repeated in other districts of the Punjab where martial law had also been introduced. In one district, an entire wedding party was arrested for breaking the curfew order and some of them were flogged. In another, students were forced to walk sixteen miles a day in the blazing sun simply to attend roll call.

But the most controversial punishment was Dyer's 'Crawling Order'. In the narrow street where the missionary, Miss Sherwood, had been beaten, Dyer ordered a whipping triangle to be erected. Soldiers were posted at each end of the street. Any Indian wanting to pass down the street had to do so on all fours. The butt-ends and bayonets of the soldiers' rifles made sure that people did not pass on their hands and knees but literally crawled on their stomachs (Nos 16–17). There were no exceptions. Rubbish gathered in the street as the road sweepers stayed away. The residents of the street, whose houses had no back entrances, were unable to go out while the soldiers were on duty between 6 am and 8 pm. Six young men, arrested on suspicion of having assaulted Miss Sherwood, were flogged at the whipping triangle before they had even been tried. Altogether about fifty people became victims of the Crawling Order before it was withdrawn on 24 April.

The Reaction in Britain and India

Dyer left Amritsar on 8 May 1919. He was confident that his action at the Jallianwala Bagh had been approved by his superiors. Just after the shooting Dyer sent a brief account to his commanding officer. He received a telegram in reply which ended with the following words: 'Your action correct and Lieutenant-Governor [Sir Michael O'Dwyer] approves.' Dyer suffered from a heart condition but it was not this that cut short his army career. Martial law was lifted in the Punjab in June 1919. The end of martial law meant also the end of press censorship which had prevented any reporting on what had happened. News of the disturbances, including the shooting at the Jallianwala Bagh and the punishments inflicted under martial law, began to filter through to the public. Indian opinion demanded an enquiry and the Government set up the Hunter Committee. As the Committee's investigations proceeded, the Government of India began to see Dyer as a liability for Britain's reputation in India. In March 1920, Dyer was relieved of his command, put on half-pay, told that no further employment would be offered to him in India and sent home to Britain (Nos 19–20).

Dyer's case and the report of the Hunter Committee raised a storm of controversy in Britain and India. In London, Parliament debated the findings of the Hunter Committee. Dyer's actions were strongly criticised by a majority of MPs in the House of Commons. But in the House of Lords a motion was passed by 129 votes to 86 which said that Dyer had not been given a fair hearing and that he had been treated unjustly (Nos 21–22). Sections of the press in Britain sprang to Dyer's defence. The *Morning Post* launched a fund to raise money for 'The Man who Saved India' (No 23). When the fund was eventually closed Dyer was a wealthy man. Over £26,000 had been raised. Fund-raising campaigns, mainly organised by women, were also started on Dyer's behalf by the European community in India (fig 7.2). Indian opinion was outaged by these expressions of sympathy and support for a man they regarded as a murderer (Nos 24–25 and fig 7.3). As a result of a resolution passed by the Indian National Congress, a trust was formed to buy the Jallianwala Bagh for the nation. What was once a scrap of wasteland is today a garden and a memorial to the victims of 13 April 1919.

DYER APPRECIATION FUND.

An appeal for funds to present
GENERAL DYER

WITH

a Sword of Honour and a Purse,

is hereby made to all
well-wishers of India,
both European and Indian,

AS A MARK OF

GRATITUDE—to General Dyer for sparing India
untold misery by arresting murder
and wholesale anarchy.

SYMPATHY—with him for the unjust sentence
passed on him.

Sympathisers are requested to form
local Committees all over India to
further the cause.

Subscriptions should be sent to the
PRESIDENT. **Dyer Appreciation
Fund**, Mussoorie, or branches of the
Allahabad and Alliance Banks, Ltd.

COMMITTEE OF WOMEN.

Mrs. E. Coughlan	Mrs. Coats	Mrs. Halliday
Mrs. Bayly	Mrs. Dunlop	Miss L. Hodgkinson
Mrs. Best	Mrs. Fowler	Mrs. Vincent Macartan
Mrs. Best	Mrs. Georges Fiet	Mrs. Millward Griffin

President—Miss Florence Holland, M. A.

7.2 British support for General Dyer. An advertisement which appeared on the front page of the Madras Mail, an English newspaper in India, 22 July 1920.

83

THE VIEWS OF SIR MICHAEL O'DWYER, LIEUTENANT -GOVERNOR OF THE PUNJAB

1. *Extract from the Report of the Congress Committee on the Punjab disturbances*

But nothing perhaps shows more clearly his dislike of the educated classes than his memorandum on the question of constitutional reforms, published together with the Government of India's despatch of March 5th 1919. Describing the demands made by the educated classes for the whole of India, he says: 'If it is clear that the demands emanate [originate] not from the mass of the people, whose interests are at stake, but from a small and quite disinterested minority, naturally enough eager for power and place [position], we must, if we are faithful to our trust, place the interests of the silent masses before the clamour [protest] of the politicians however troublesome and insistent.'

INDIA'S CONTRIBUTION TO THE FIRST WORLD WAR

2. *Numbers of Indians serving in all theatres of the war*

	COMBATANTS		Non-combatants	TOTAL
	Indian officers and Warrant officers	Indian other ranks		
To France	1,911	82,974	47,611	132,496
To East Africa	826	33,633	12,477	46,906
To Mesopotamia	7,812	287,753	293,152	588,717
To Egypt	1,889	94,596	19,674	116,159
To Gallipoli	90	3,003	1,335	4,428
To Salonika	31	3,643	1,264	4,938
To Aden	343	15,655	4,245	20,243
To Persian Gulf	615	17,537	11,305	29,457
TOTAL	13,517	538,794	391,003	943,344

THE PARLIAMENTARY SCALES OF BRITISH JUSTICE.

[The Dyer-hards in the Lords have triumphed. They have succeeded in widening the gaping wound in the heart of poor Punjab.]

7.3 A cartoon from Hindi Punch, July 1920, demonstrating the Indian nationalist view of the Dyer debate in the House of Lords.

85

3. Message from Mr Lloyd George, the Prime Minister, to the Viceroy, Lord Chelmsford, 21 March 1917

I wish on behalf of the British Government to express to the Government and the people of India our most sincere gratitude for the magnificent contribution [of £100 millions] which India has just made to financing the War. Coming in addition to the enthusiasm and loyalty manifested throughout India on the outbreak of the war and to the invaluable services since rendered by the Indian Army, this gift is to us a living proof that India shares wholeheartedly with the other subjects of the Crown in the ideals for which we are fighting this war. That India should come forward of her own accord in this crisis and render such real and opportune [timely] assistance is not only a source of sincere satisfaction to His Majesty's Government, but must produce a better mutual understanding among all the resources and peoples under the British Crown.

THE RIOTS AT AMRITSAR

4. Mr Miles Irving, Deputy Commissioner, Amritsar, giving evidence before the Hunter Committee

Q. Would it be consistent with the facts as you know them, to regard the outbreak of the 10th April as the case of protest against the deportations of Drs Kitchlew and Satyapal which spontaneously developed into mob violence, marked by murder and incendiarism [arson]?
A. I think that is a very good account. It spontaneously developed. It flared up in a moment. I don't think people went out with that design.

THE ATTACKS ON COMMUNICATIONS

5. Hunter Committee: Majority Report

The attacks on communications were in many cases motivated by sheer *anti*-Government feeling. The railway is considered, quite rightly, a Government institution and railway damage is in these cases simply a part of the destruction of Government property upon which the mobs were bent. There is, however, an additional motive present apparently in a large number of cases in the desire, if possible, to prevent the arrival of troops and to make calls for assistance impossible.

6. *Hunter Committee: Minority Report*

While the attacks on communications look formidable by their mere numbers, some of them were of a very trivial character. No doubt, there had been the cutting of telegraph wires and the burning of railway stations; but the result of all this in crippling the means of communications was not as great as at first sight it might appear. The Agent of the North-Western Railway in an appendix to his report, dated the 2nd July 1919, sums up the situation as follows: 'The effect of the disturbance was to paralyse the railway as a commercial system for the period say 10th to 21st April; as an instrument of Government administration for transport the railway was not paralysed. The outbreak in this respect signally failed.' ... It must also be borne in mind that the largely operative reason for cutting the railway line was to stop the goods trains and secure loot.

THE PUNJAB DISTURBANCES: RIOT OR REBELLION?

7. *Hunter Committee: Majority Report*

On the evidence before us there is nothing to show that the outbreak in the Punjab was part of a pre-arranged conspiracy to overthrow the British Government in India by force ... But the general teaching of the doctrine of civil disobedience to laws to masses of uneducated men must inevitably lead to a breach of the peace and disorder ... In the situation as it presented itself day by day to the Punjab Government, there were grounds for the gravest anxiety. It was difficult, probably unsafe, for the authorities not to assume that the outbreak was the result of a definite organisation ... a movement which had started in rioting and became a rebellion might have rapidly developed into a revolution.

8. *Hunter Committee: Minority Report*

On the evidence before us we are of the opinion, that there was no rebellion ... nor any organisation for that purpose; further there was no organisation even for bringing about the disturbances and the atrocities which were committed by the mobs seized by the frenzy of the moment ... The first circumstance that invites attention in this connection is that in no place were the mobs provided with fire-arms or swords or other weapons of that character ... at no time was any attempt made by the crowds to obtain arms by raiding the houses of license holders or the ammunition shops in the disturbed areas.

9. *Sir Michael O'Dwyer, Lieutenant-Governor of the Punjab, giving evidence before the Hunter Committee*

Q. In your statement at page 10 you indicate the view that there was an organisation – a widespread organisation – on the 15th April. Your suggestion is that the whole country was involved. Do you still adhere to that or not?

A. There were similar and simultaneous outbreaks in various parts of India as far apart as Bombay, Ahmedabad, and Calcutta ...

Q. Where was this central organisation?

A. I have no proof of it. But I am strongly inclined to believe that it did exist. There was some organisation ...

Q. You have no evidence in support of this?

A. I cannot give it. As I say, I left the province directly after these disorders were put down and did not have the opportunity of investigating the matter further.

10. *Report of the Committee of the Indian National Congress*

The people of the Punjab were incensed [made angry] against Sir Michael O'Dwyer's administration by reason of his studied [deliberate] contempt and distrust of the educated classes ... The Rowlatt agitation disturbed the public mind and shook public confidence in the good will of the Government ... There was no conspiracy to overthrow the Government of the Punjab ... The arrests and deportations of Drs Kitchlew and Satyapal were unjustifiable and were the only direct cause of hysterical popular excitment ... Whatever the cause of provocation, the mob excesses are deeply to be regretted and condemned.

THE MEETING AT THE JALLIANWALA BAGH ON THE DAY OF THE SHOOTING

11. *Sir Michael O'Dwyer, giving evidence before the Hunter Committee*

All communications from Amritsar had been torn up, both railways and telegraph ... and a train had been derailed and looted close by that morning. Therefore the population of Amritsar and the people who gathered at the Jallianwala Bagh ... were aware of the fact that there was a rebellion on foot, that the Government was taking steps ... to crush that rebellion, and that ... the first thing the Government had to do was to prevent any large gathering of people ... the great mass of the people knew or must have known that day when they went to the Jallianwala Bagh that they were going there in defiance of the proclamation ... and at the risk of their life.

12. Hunter Committee: Minority Report

It is clear that there must have been a considerable number of people who were perfectly innocent and who had never in all probability heard of the proclamation. The Punjab Government in their case submitted to us say that 'there were a considerable number of peasants present at the Jallianwala Bagh meeting ... but they were there for other than political reasons.' ... It is therefore obvious that the crowd ... comprised people who did not belong to the city of Amritsar at all, and who therefore cannot ... be held responsible for the acts of the hooligans on 10th April.

THE SHOOTING AT THE JALLIANWALA BAGH

13. General Dyer's written report, 25 August 1919

I fired and continued to fire until the crowd dispersed and I consider this the least amount of firing which would produce the necessary moral and widespread effect, it was my duty to produce if I was to justify my action. If more troops had been at hand the casualties would have been greater in proportion. *It was no longer a question of merely dispersing the crowd*; but one of producing a sufficient moral effect, from a military point of view, not only on those who were present but more specifically throughout the Punjab. There could be no question of undue severity.

14. General Dyer giving evidence before the Hunter Committee

Q. When you got into the Jallianwala Bagh what did you do?
A. I opened fire.
Q. At once?
A. Immediately. I had thought about the matter, and it did not take me more than 30 seconds to make up my mind as to what my duty was ...
Q. What reason had you to suppose that if you had ordered the assembly to leave the Bagh they would not have done so without the necessity of your firing, continued firing for a length of time?
A. Yes; I think it quite possible that I could have dispersed them perhaps even without firing.
Q. Why did you not adopt that course?
A. I could not disperse them for some time; then they would all come back and laugh at me, and I considered I would be making myself a fool ...
Q. I take it that your idea in taking that action was to strike terror?
A. Call it what you like. I was going to punish them. My idea from a military point of view was to make a wide impression.

15. *An eye-witness account, from the Congress Report on the Punjab disturbances*

We must now supply further details of the scene from the mouths of eye-witnesses. We have already adverted [referred] to Lala Girdhari Lal's statement. He happened to watch the scene from a house overlooking the Bagh. 'I saw hundreds of people killed on the spot. The worst part of the whole thing was that the firing was directed towards the gates through which the people were running out. There were small outlets, 4 or 5 in all, and bullets rained over the people at all these gates, and ... many got trampled under the feet of the rushing crowds and thus lost their lives. Blood was pouring in profusion. Even those who lay flat on the ground were shot ... No arrangements were made by the authorities to look after the dead or wounded ... I then gave water to the wounded and rendered such assistance as was possible ... I went round the whole place and saw almost every body lying there. There were heaps of them at different places ... The dead bodies were of grown up people and young boys also. Some had their heads cut open, others had eyes shot, and nose, chest, arms or legs shattered ... I think there must have been over 1,000 dead bodies in the garden then ... I saw people were hurrying up and many had to leave their dead and wounded, because they were afraid of being fired on again after 8 pm.'

MARTIAL LAW IN AMRITSAR

16. *General Dyer explains his Crawling Order to the Hunter Committee*

I felt a woman had been beaten. We look upon women as sacred or ought to. I was searching my brain for a suitable punishment to meet this awful case ... I felt the street ought to be looked upon as sacred ... Therefore I posted a couple of pickets and I told them no Indians were to pass along there. I then also said that if they had to pass, they must go on all fours. It never entered my brain that any sensible or sane man under those conditions would intentionally go through that street.

17. *Kahan Chand, an Indian victim of the Crawling Order*

I have been blind for the last twenty years ... About 18th April, while I was groping my way into the street with the support of a stick that I always carry, I was asked by a policeman to halt. On my begging him to let me proceed, I was told that I could only do so if I was willing to crawl on my belly, and had hardly gone a few yards when I received a kick on my back, and my stick slipped out of my hands ...

THE VERDICTS OF THE HUNTER AND CONGRESS COMMITTEES

18. Hunter Committee: Majority Report

General Dyer's action in firing on the crowd at the Jallianwala Bagh is open to criticism in two respects. (First) that he started firing without giving the people who had assembled a chance to disperse, and (second) that he continued firing for a substantial period of time after the crowd had commenced to disperse.

19. Hunter Committee: Minority Report

General Dyer wanted by his action at the Jallianwala Bagh to create a 'wide impression' and 'a great moral effect'. We have no doubt that he did succeed in creating a very wide impression and a great moral effect, but of a character quite opposite to the one he intended. The story of this indiscriminate killing of innocent people not engaged in committing any acts of violence, but assembled in a meeting, has undoubtedly produced such a deep impression throughout the length and breadth of the country, so prejudicial [damaging] to the British Government that it would take a good deal and a long time to rub it out. The action of general Dyer, as well as some acts of the martial law administration ... have been compared to the acts of 'frightfulness' committed by some of the German military commanders during the war in Belgium and France.

20. Report of the Committee of the Indian National Congress

No provocation whatever was given to the Military Authorities and nothing, either in Amritsar or outside it, justified the massacre. It was a calculated act of inhumanity, and if the British Rule in India is to be purged of this inexcusable wrong, General Dyer must be immediately relieved of his command and brought to justice.

THE REACTION IN BRITAIN AND INDIA

21. Winston Churchill, speaking during the debate in the House of Commons, 8 July 1920

[O]ne tremendous fact stands out – I mean the slaughter of nearly 400 persons and the wounding of probably three or four times as many, at the Jallianwala Bagh on 13th April. That is an episode which appears to me without precedent or parallel in the modern history of the British Empire ... It is an extraordinary event, a monstrous event, an event which stands in singular and sinister isolation.

22. *Lord Sumner, speaking during the debate in the House of Lords, 20 July 1920*

You are weakening the hands of every one of those officers if you let it be understood from the precedent of General Dyer that they will not afterwards get, I do not say support, but a fair consideration of all the difficulties and dangers to which they themselves are exposed ... You have to use force if it is necessary and it is agreed that it was necessary.

23. *Report in the Morning Post, 8 July 1920*

A great wrong is being done to a man who has served his country well – who, by his courage and decision in a moment of dangerous crisis, averted an immeasurable calamity. For this service the reward is a broken career ... While General Dyer saved India, the politicians are saving themselves at his expense ... General Dyer ... is not only broken, but financially crippled ... We forthwith propose to open a General Dyer fund, the subscriptions to which ... will give him, in his hour of bitterness and tribulation, an assurance that some of his fellow-countrymen at least extend to him their sympathy, their confidence, and their gratitude ... Subscriptions should be addressed to the Editor of the *Morning Post*, and marked 'General Dyer Fund', and will be acknowledged from day to day in these columns.

24. *Rabindranath Tagore, as reported in the Hindu Weekly newspaper, 29 July 1920. Tagore was India's leading poet. He won the Nobel Prize for Literature in 1913. He was knighted in 1915 but gave up the honour because of British support for General Dyer*

LONDON, JULY 21 – On the afternoon following the close of the Dyer debate in the Lords, I asked Dr Rabindranath Tagore what he thought of the situation. Speaking with the deepest emotion he said ... he felt grieved and insulted at the unashamed condonation [support] of a brutal outrage by the very class from which our rulers are recruited. This makes us, he said, realise the futility and humiliation of relying on any boon [favour] of any value from those who hold us in contempt ... The present shock ... if accepted in the right spirit will prove a blessing in disguise and form the basis of a new era of a career of national self-respect ...

25. *Jawaharlal Nehru, writing in his Autobiography in 1936*

Towards the end of that year (1919) I travelled from Amritsar to Delhi by the night train ... In the morning I discovered that all my fellow-passengers were military officers ... One of them was holding forth in an aggressive and triumphant tone and soon I discovered that he was Dyer, the hero of the Jallianwala Bagh, and he was describing his Amritsar experiences. He pointed out how he had had the whole town at his mercy and he had felt like reducing the rebellious city to a heap of ashes, but he took pity on it and refrained ... I was greatly shocked to hear his conversation and to observe his callous [unfeeling] manner.

CHAPTER EIGHT

GANDHI AND CIVIL DISOBEDIENCE

His early life

Mohandas Karamchand Gandhi was born in 1869 in the small princely state of Porbandar in Western India. As a young boy he was shy and nervous. He often ran home from school to avoid speaking to other children for fear that they might make fun of him. Gandhi was married at the age of fourteen. Four years later he went alone to London to study law. Lonely and unhappy at first, he tried to adapt to his new surroundings by becoming an Edwardian English gentleman. He bought an evening suit and top hat, took dancing lessons and spent £3 on a violin. The expense became too much. He gave up his attempt to become a gentleman and settled for a more modest lifesyle. He spent no more than sixpence on his three daily meals. When he returned to India in 1890 he struggled to make a living in his chosen legal career. In 1893 he accepted an offer to represent a firm of wealthy Indian merchants who were involved in a court case in South Africa.

South Africa and *Satyagraha*

South Africa was the making of Gandhi. He intended to stay for one year and travelled out as an unsuccessful lawyer totally lacking in self-confidence. He returned to India twenty-one years later with a reputation as a political leader. Soon after his arrival in South Africa, Gandhi became the victim of racial discrimination. He was thrown out of a first-class railway carriage because of the colour of his skin. Realising that his fellow-countrymen suffered much worse humiliation every day of their lives, Gandhi decided to stay on to help them. The majority were contract labourers who worked on the plantations and in the mines. But they also included a number of merchants, many of whom were Muslims. South Africa therefore gave Gandhi valuable experience of working with different communities. His work on behalf of the Indian community was at first conducted as a barrister in the law courts and he became quite wealthy as a result. But in time he rejected his wordly possessions and dedicated himself to accept a life of simplicity. He established settlements which became experiments in community living where everyone shared in the most menial tasks. He also developed his strategy of *satyagraha*. 'Passive resistance' was how many defined *satyagraha* but Gandhi himself preferred to call it 'truth-force' or 'soul-force'. The idea was to oppose unjust laws, not by violent protest, but by deliberately breaking them in a peaceful manner and inviting the penalty for so doing. By displaying a willingness to undergo personal suffering, Gandhi believed that, in time, the law-enforcer would come to accept the justice of the law-breaker's cause. Gandhi was arrested on three occasions in South Africa. He once appeared in court with handcuffs on his wrists and chains on his ankles. In prison he was set to work breaking stones.

Gandhi as a 'loyal' British subject

When he returned to India in 1915, Gandhi was not at first a critic of the British empire. During the Boer War in South Africa at the turn of the century his sympathies had been with the Boers but he organised an Indian Volunteer Ambulance Corps to help the British. When war broke out in Europe in 1914, Gandhi was on a visit to London. Together with a number of Indians who were living in Britain he again offered his services to the Empire and when he returned to India he took part in recruitment campaigns for the army (Nos 1–2). Gandhi's 'loyal' services were recognised when he received a number of British honours. These included the *Kaiser-i-Hind* (Emperor of India) Gold Medal which was awarded in 1915 in recognition of his humanitarian work in South Africa.

Gandhi in opposition to British rule in India

But Gandhi's trust in the British was broken by events at the end of the First World War. He led a protest movement against the Rowlatt Act of 1919 and served on the Congress Committee which investigated the Punjab disturbances and the Amritsar Massacre (see chapter 7). Like many of his countrymen, he was shocked by the efforts made in certain British circles to defend General Dyer. He was also angry that many other British officials who had committed acts of cruelty under martial law elsewhere in the Punjab had gone completely unpunished.

To gather support for a major protest campaign against the British Government, Gandhi joined forces with the Khilafat movement. Organised by some of India's Muslim leaders, the Khilafat movement had been established at the end of the war in protest against allied plans to break up the defeated Turkish empire. India's Muslim leaders were particularly concerned at allied plans to reduce the authority of the Turkish Khalifah. The Khalifah was the name given to the Turkish Sultan in his capacity as a religious leader. Throughout India, many Muslims regarded the Khalifah as their main religious leader. Amritsar and the Khilafat question persuaded Gandhi to return all the medals which had been awarded to him by the British. They also converted him into a determined opponent of continued British rule in India (No 3).

The Non-Cooperation Movement

Over the next twenty years, Gandhi led the Indian National Congress in three major campaigns against the British government. His campaigns began in 1920 with the non-cooperation movement. Gandhi planned non-cooperation as a series of escalating measures. If carried out to the full, Gandhi declared that these measures would enable India to achieve *swaraj* (self-government) within a year. At the beginning, Indians who held British titles were asked to resign them. Students and their parents were asked to boycott government schools. Lawyers were asked to give up their jobs and devote themselves to public service. Then, Indian members of the civil services were asked to resign from their jobs and Indian politicians were urged to boycott the elections for the new legislative councils. Finally, as measures of last resort, Indian members of the police and armed forces were asked to resign and selected Congress members were instructed to organise peasant movements for the non-payment of taxes. Outbreaks of violence, which culminated in a mob setting fire to a police station and burning alive twenty-two policemen, persuaded Gandhi to call a halt to the non-cooperation movement in February 1922. He was arrested in March, put on trial and given a six-year prison sentence. He was released after two years on the grounds of ill-health (Nos 4–8).

The Civil Disobedience Movement

Gandhi's next major campaign was the civil disobedience movement which began in 1930 with the famous 'salt march' (fig 8.1). Gandhi was arrested but released in January 1931 for talks with the Viceroy, Lord Irwin. He agreed to a truce in the Gandhi–Irwin pact of

Newspaper report on the commencement
of Dandi March, March 12, 1930.

I want world
sympathy in
this battle of
Right against
might.

sd. M.K. Gandhi

5ʰ.4.'30

A message from Gandhi
Gandhi and fellow *satyagrahis* on the march

8.1 *The Civil Disobedience movement. A message from Gandhi at the beginning of the salt march,*
March–April 1930.

March 1931. Civil disobedience was suspended and Gandhi travelled to London to attend the second in a series of round table conferences. The conferences had been called by the British Government to consider the next stage of reforms on India's road towards self-government. The Indian National Congress had boycotted the first conference and no agreement was reached when Gandhi attended the second (fig 8.2). Gandhi returned to India at the end of 1931 and instructed his followers to resume civil disobedience. He was again arrested and remained in prison until civil disobedience was finally brought to an end in 1934 (Nos 9–12).

The Quit India Movement

Gandhi's last major campaign was the Quit India movement of 1942. Launched at a time when Britain was at war with both Germany and Japan, the British viewed the Quit India movement as an act of treachery. The Indian National Congress was outlawed and its leaders arrested. Gandhi remained in detention until 1944 (No 13).

Gandhi as a social and economic reformer

Throughout these years of political struggle aginst the British, Gandhi was equally active as a social and economic reformer. He campaigned in particular to improve the status of India's Untouchable community and described the Untouchables as *Harijan*s (Children of God). He also believed in self-sufficiency and led by example, devoting part of each day to spinning *khadi* (home-made cloth). For Gandhi, the spinning wheel represented the simplicity of life in an Indian village (fig 8.3). It was a way of life he wanted to preserve and improve upon. He had little time for modern industrial society as it had developed in the West. In his eyes, industrialisation bred exploitation, greed and squalor.

The Hindu–Muslim question and Gandhi's assassination

Gandhi's other major concern – to bridge the growing gap between Hindus and Muslims – eventually cost him his life. When he was released from detention in 1944, Gandhi struggled in vain to overcome the forces moving India towards partition and the creation of a separate Muslim state of Pakistan. When partition came in 1947 it was marked by widespread violence, particularly in the divided province of the Punjab. Gandhi's appeals

INSOLENT BILL OF RIGHTS.

CHALLENGE THAT MUST BE ANSWERED.

India Will Be Lost Unless Conservatives Make a Strong Stand.

ACTION of the utmost gravity was taken against the British Empire yesterday by Gandhi and his fellow-members of the All-India Congress at Karachi.

They passed resolutions demanding that Indians shall have:

The right to carry firearms,
Power to exclude all foreign cloth and yarn,
Full social and commercial equality with Britons, and
Full control of India's finances, army, key industries, and foreign affairs.

This is a direct challenge to British rule, a throwing down of the gauntlet to the British nation, a turning point in the history of India and the Empire.

If this challenge is not taken up it can only mean that India will be lost to the Empire.

The only party capable of taking the initiative in this matter is the Conservative Party.

Its members must take a strong line and insist that the time has come to call a halt to the disastrous and perilous policy of surrender. THE CONSERVATIVE PARTY MUST MAKE A FIRM AND DETERMINED STAND.

LED BY EXTREMISTS.

GANDHI LOSES HIS FEAR OF BRITISH ANTAGONISM.

From OUR SPECIAL CORRESPONDENT, SIR PERCIVAL PHILLIPS.

KARACHI, Tuesday.

GANDHI'S mandate to the next Round-Table Conference is embodied in resolutions passed by Congress to-night which make new and amazing demands to Britain.

They insist not only on India's complete independence, with control of the army, militia, and foreign affairs, but also on

The reduction of Britain's military expenditure in India by at least 50 per cent.,

A maximum of £500 a year for salaries of Government servants,

The right of all Indians to carry firearms, and

Complete social and commercial equality with British residents in India.

This extraordinary "Bill of Rights" in which Gandhi and the Pandit Jawarhalal Nehru, the extremist friend of Moscow, have collaborated, shows a strong impress of the Soviet doctrines which Nehru desires to adopt in the new India.

It insists on the

Termination of the "exploitation of the masses";
"Religious neutrality" on the part of the State;
Labour to be freed from "serfdom," with the right to form unions;
Large reduction in land revenue, rent, and taxes;
Adult suffrage.
Free primary education;
Progressive income tax;
The official exclusion of foreign cloth and yarn;
No duty on salt; and
Control by the State of key industries and mineral resources.

GANDHI WON OVER.

Many of these impudent demands were introduced by Gandhi to placate Nehru's extremists. I understand that at first he was not willing to put forward such a sweeping programme of independence, believing that it would arouse antagonism in Britain even among the present supporters of the movement for self-government, but he was persuaded to submit it to the Subjects Committee, which passed it by a safe majority, thereby giving the mahatma the assurance that he would have the backing of Congress.

The spirit of self-confidence in the Congress camp is very high to-night. The speeches of the last few days have convinced the delegates that they really have Britain in full retreat and that now is the time to put on the fullest possible pressure.

8.2 The second Round Table Conference in London in 1931. This cutting from the Daily Mail, 1 April 1931, explains why no agreement was possible between Gandhi and the British Government.

and fasts for peace between the warring communities, together with his defence of the rights of those Muslims left behind in India, provoked his assassination by a Hindu extremist in January 1948.

An assessment of Gandhi

How great was Gandhi's achievement and how lasting his influence? In several respects, Gandhi failed in what he set out to achieve. His lifelong political ambition that India would become free but remain united was destroyed by partition in 1947. Despite his support for the Khilafat movement and the efforts he later made to promote Hindu–Muslim unity, Gandhi never gained the trust and confidence of the Muslims. His life and ideas were so closely bound up with Hindu influences that to many Muslims he represented the threat of Hindu domination (No 14). The Hindu–Muslim question is examined in more detail in chapter 9.

Also, beyond a small and devoted band of personal followers, Gandhi's belief in non-violence and his vision of India's future gained few converts. For Gandhi, non-violence was an act of faith but for the majority of the Indian nationalists it was merely a tactical weapon (No 8). Looking to the future, Gandhi wanted India to become a country of self-supporting villages. There would be little need for government in the modern sense with huge government departments employing vast armies of civil servants. Gandhi wanted Congress to give a lead, not as a party of governmment, but as a movement dedicated to social and educational reform. However, since independence in 1947, India has developed along different lines. People have left the villages to work in the towns, the country has become industrialised, the state has played an ever increasing role in the lives of the people and Congress has developed into India's major party of government (Nos 15–16).

On the other hand, there can be no denying that during his lifetime Gandhi had an enormous appeal for the mass of the Indian people. To the millions of peasants he was the *Mahatma* or 'Great Soul'. To his closest friends he was *bapu* (father) or Gandhiji. Adding 'ji' to the end of a person's name is an Indian way of indicating affection and respect (Nos 17–18).

Gandhi also played a major role in the reorganisation of the Indian National Congress which took place in 1920. A new Congress constitution was adopted in that year. Of the many changes introduced, one of the most significant was the establishment of Congress Committees in the districts of British India. As a result, Congress was now organised on a national basis and it had a much broader basis of support. It became more

8.3 Gandhi with Jawaharlal Nehru at a spinning session in 1946. Nehru did not agree with Gandhi's ideas about how Indian society should be organised and the Indian economy managed once India became independent.

like a political party. Members paid subscription fees and elected delegates to an All-India Congress Committee. Gandhi's Congress was never a tightly knit party consisting of like-minded men and women sharing similar objectives. It was often a divided party. Regional differences were always important. The interests of the Congress leaders at national level often clashed with those of the local leaders in the provinces. Political opinions within Congress varied enormously. Moderates and conservatives rubbed shoulders with radicals and socialists (No 19). Keeping such a party together for as long as he did was another of Gandhi's achievements.

Finally, since his death in 1948, Gandhi's influence has been seen in various parts of the world. People struggling for freedom and independence have usually resorted to revolution and violence. But others have chosen the path of non-violence and have paid tributes to the example set by Gandhi (Nos 20–21). In the modern world today, passive resistance in any form owes something to the ideas of Gandhi.

GANDHI AS A 'LOYAL' BRITISH SUBJECT

1. Gandhi explains his support for Britain at the time of the Boer War in South Africa

When the war was declared, my personal sympathies were all with the Boers, but I believed then that I had yet no right in such cases to enforce my individual convictions [beliefs] ... Suffice it to say that my loyalty to the British rule drove me to participation with the British in that war. I felt that, if I demanded rights as a British citizen, it was also my duty, as such, to participate in the defence of the British Empire. I held then that India could achieve her complete emancipation [freedom] only within and through the British Empire. So I collected together as many comrades as possible, and with very great difficulty got their services accepted as an ambulance corps.

2. Gandhi explains his support for Britain during the First World War

I felt that Indians residing in England ought to do their bit in the war. English students had volunteered to serve in the army, and Indians might do no less. A number of objections were taken to this line of argument. There was, it was contended [suggested], a world of difference between the Indians and the English. We were slaves and they were masters. How could a slave co-operate with the master in the hour of the latter's need? Was it not the duty of the slave, seeking to be free, to make the master's need his opportunity? This argument failed to appeal to me then. I knew the difference of status between an Indian and Englishman, but I did not believe that we had been quite reduced to slavery. I felt then that it was more the fault of individual British officials than of the British system, and that we could convert them by love. If we would improve our status through the help and co-operation of the British, it was our duty to win their help by standing by them in their hour of need.

GANDHI BECOMES AN OPPONENT OF BRITISH RULE IN INDIA

3. Article by Gandhi in his newspaper, Young India, 28 July 1920

I sincerely believed that the Mussulman [Muslim] sentiment would be placated [calmed] and that the officers that had misbehaved during the martial law regime in the Punjab would at least be dismissed and the people would be otherwise made to feel that a Government that had always been found quick (and rightly) to punish popular excesses [wrong-doings] would not fail to punish its agents' misdeeds. But to my amazement and dismay, I have discovered that the present representatives of the Empire have become dishonest and unscrupulous. They have no real regard for the wishes of the people of India and they count Indian honour as of little consequence. I can no longer retain affection for a Government so evilly manned as it is now-a-days.

THE NON-COOPERATION MOVEMENT

4. *Lord Reading was Viceroy (1921–26) during the non-cooperation movement. In this letter dated 19 May 1921 to Edwin Montagu, the Secretary of State for India, Reading recorded his impressions of Gandhi*

There is nothing striking about his appearance. He came to visit me in a white *dhoti* (waistcloth) and cap, woven on a spinning wheel, with bare feet and legs, and my first impression on seeing him ushered into my room was that there was nothing to arrest attention in his appearance, and that I should have passed him by in the street without a second look at him. When he talks the impression is different. He is direct and expresses himself well in excellent English with a fine appreciation of the value of the words he uses. There is no hesitation about him and there is a ring of sincerity in all that he utters, save when discussing some political questions. His religious views are, I believe, genuinely held and he is convinced to a point almost bordering on fanaticism that non-violence and love will give India its independence and enable it to withstand the British Government. His religious and moral views are admirable ... but I confess that I find it difficult to understand his practice of them in politics. To put it quite briefly, he is like the rest of us, when engaged in a political movement he wishes to gather all under his umbrella and to reform them and bring them to his views. He has consequently to accept many with whom he is not in accord [agreement], and has to do his best to keep the combination together.

5. *For some of the older and more moderate members of the Indian National Congress, non-cooperation involved heavy sacrifices. In this extract from his Autobiography, Jawaharlal Nehru recorded the dilemmas facing his father Motilal Nehru, one of India's most famous lawyers*

I saw very little of father in those days ... But whenever I met him, I noticed how he was continually grappling [struggling] with this problem. Quite apart from the national aspect of the question there was the personal aspect. Non-cooperation meant his withdrawing from legal practice; it meant a total break from his past life and a new fashioning of it – not an easy matter when one is on the eve of one's sixtieth birthday. It was a break from old political colleagues, from his profession, from the social life to which he had grown accustomed, and a giving up of many an expensive habit which he had grown into. For the financial aspect of the question was not an unimportant one, and it was obvious that he would have to reduce his standard of living if his income from his profession vanished. But his reason, his strong sense of self-respect, and his pride, all led him step by step to throw in his lot wholeheartedly with the new movement.

6. *Many of the Congress moderates were not prepared to follow Gandhi. Sir Dinshaw Edulji Wacha, who had been Congress President in 1901, summed up his feelings about Gandhi in this letter to a colleague dated 6 October 1920*

I never gave Gandhi credit for even an iota [one bit] of political sagacity [wisdom] ... The man is full of overweening [arrogant] conceit and personal ambition and the vast unthinking multitude ... seem to be quite mad ... in following like a flock of sheep, this unsafe shepherd who is bringing the country on the very brink of chaos and anarchy. And your people were for a time so *enthused* [enthusiastic] and worshipped him as if he were a mortal god on earth. Time, time, time, will be the avenger of the wrongs this madman is now inflicting on the poor country in his mad and arrogant career.

7. *Gandhi's influence during the non-cooperation movement, as reported in a letter from Lord Reading to Mr Montagu, 6 October 1921*

Gandhi is undoubtedly a very potent [strong] influence; he has the advantage of the religious worship of vast crowds of people who know nothing of politics and who accept everything that falls from him as gospel truth. True it is that he has proved wrong in various political prophecies and that he has failed to implement his promise of *swaraj* [self-government] within the time limited by him; nevertheless the people believe in him as a holy man; they may have doubts, at least among the thinking portion of his following whether he can carry out his policy; but they are prepared blindly to follow him and take the chance of it.

8. *Outbreaks of violence persuaded Gandhi to call off the non-cooperation movement in February 1922. The most serious occurred when a mob set fire to a police station and burned alive twenty-two policemen at the remote village of Chauri Chaura in the United Provinces. Writing in his Autobiography, Jawaharlal Nehru recalled the sense of frustration at Gandhi's decision*

The sudden suspension of our movement after the Chauri Chaura incident was resented ... Chauri Chaura may have been and was a deplorable occurrence and wholly opposed to the spirit of the non-violent movement; but were a remote village and a mob of excited peasants in an out-of-the-way place going to put an end, for some time at least, to our national struggle for freedom? If this was the inevitable consequence of a sporadic [isolated] act of violence, then surely there was something lacking in the technique of a non-violent struggle. For it seemed to us to be impossible to guarantee against the occurrence of some such untoward [unexpected] incident. Must we train the three hundred and odd millions of India in the thoery and practice of non-violent action before we could go forward? [F]or the National Congress as a whole the non-violent method was not, and could not be, a religion ... It could only be a policy and a method promising certain results, and by those results it would have to be finally judged.

THE CIVIL DISOBEDIENCE MOVEMENT

9. *The Civil Disobedience movement began when Lord Irwin was Viceroy (1926–31). Irwin met Gandhi for the first time in 1927. In this letter to his father, Viscount Halifax, dated 6 November 1927, Irwin recorded his impressions of Gandhi*

[I] have broken the ice and met Gandhi. He really is an interesting personality. Of course his political position is that England and the British Parliament have no moral claim to be the judges of Indian progress ...and he struck me as singularly [remarkably] remote from practical politics. It was rather like talking to someone who had stepped off one planet on to this for a short visit of a fortnight, and whose whole mental outlook was quite other to that which was regulating most of the affairs on the planet to which he had descended.

10. *On 2 March 1930, on the eve of his salt march, Gandhi wrote the following letter to Lord Irwin*

Dear Friend

Before embarking on Civil Disobedience and taking the risk I have dreaded to take all these years, I would fain [gladly] approach you and find a way out.

I must not be misunderstood. Though I hold the British rule in India to be a curse, I do not, therefore, consider Englishmen in general to be worse than any other people on earth. I have the privilege of claiming many Englishmen as dearest friends ...

And why do I regard the British rule as a curse?

It has impoverished the dumb millions by a system of progressive exploitation and by a ruinously expensive military and civil administration which the country can never afford. It has reduced us politically to serfdom. It has sapped [undermimed] the foundations of our culture.

The *ryot* [peasant] has remained as helpless as ever ... Even the salt he must use to live is so taxed as to make the burden fall heaviest on him ... The tax shows itself still more burdensome on the poor man when it is remembered that salt is the one thing he must eat more than the rich man both individually and collectively ...

I know that in embarking on non-violence I shall be running what might fairly be termed a mad risk. But the victories of truth have never been won without risks, often of the gravest character. Conversion of a nation that has consciously or unconsciously preyed upon another, far more numerous, far more ancient and no less cultured than itself, is worth any amount of risk.

I have deliberately used the word conversion. For my ambition is no less than to convert the British people, through non-violence, and thus make them see the wrong they have done to India. I do not seek to harm your people …

[I]f you cannot see your way to deal with these evils and my letter makes no appeal to your heart, on the 11th day of this month, I shall proceed with such co-workers of the Ashram [spiritual retreat] as I can take, to disregard the provisions of the salt laws. I regard this tax to be the most iniquitous [wicked] of all from the poor man's standpoint. As the Independence movement is essentially for the poorest in the land the beginning will be made with this evil. The wonder is that we have submitted to the cruel monopoly for so long. It is, I know, open to you to frustrate my design by arresting me. I hope that there will be tens of thousands ready, in a disciplined manner, to take up the work after me, and, in the act of disobeying the salt act, to lay themselves open to the penalties of a law that should never have disfigured the Statute [Law] Book …

I remain
Your sincere friend
M K Gandhi

11. Gandhi's salt march captured the popular imagination in India, as Jawaharal Nehru recalled in his Autobiography

It seemed as though a spring had suddenly been released; and all over the country, in town and village, salt manufacture was the topic of the day, and so many curious expedients [devices] were adopted to produce salt. We knew precious little about it, and so we read it up where we could, and issued leaflets giving directions, and collected pots and pans and ultimately succeeded in producing some unwholesome stuff, which we waved in triumph, and often auctioned for fancy prices. It was really immaterial [unimportant] whether the stuff was good or bad; the main thing was to commit a breach of the obnoxious [hated] Salt Law, and we were successful in that, even though the quality of our salt was poor. As we saw the abounding enthusiasm of the people and the way salt-making was spreading like a prairie fire, we felt a little ashamed for having questioned the efficacy [effectiveness] of this method when it was first proposed by Gandhiji. And we marvelled at the amazing knack of the man to impress the mutitude and make it act in an organised way.

12. Lord Irwin, in letters to his father on the question of whether or not Gandhi should be arrested

7 April 1930. I am anxious to avoid arresting Gandhi if I can without letting a 'Gandhi legend' establish itself that we are afraid to lay hands on him. This we clearly cannot afford. But at present there are no signs of that idea obtaining currency [becoming widely accepted]. Apart from this, there is the undoubted fact that he is generally regarded as a great religious leader rather than a politician and that his arrest, while it will certainly not make the world fall in half, would yet offend the sentiment of many who disagree with him and his policy in reason, and also would not achieve the purpose that would be achieved if his movement could of itself appear futile and ridiculous.

23 April 1930. All my political business is very engrossing and troublesome. The big question is whether or not Gandhi should be arrested. I have no doubt that we were right not to arrest him to begin with, but latterly [of late] I must confess my doubts have been growing. I have an uneasy feeling that a legend is growing up that he is unarrestable, which of course is very bad, and I find my mind moving to a conviction that it is necessary to break it. This also will make trouble if we do it, and it is not an easy thing to strike the balance.

THE LEGACY OF THE QUIT INDIA MOVEMENT

13. Field Marshal Wavell was Commander-in-Chief of the Army in India when Gandhi began the Quit India movement in 1942. With Britain at war, Wavell regarded Quit India as an act of treachery. From 1943–46, as Lord Wavell, he served as Viceroy. His attitude towards Gandhi continued to be influenced by the Quit India Movement. In 1946, a Cabinet Mission was sent to India from Britain. The Mission carried proposals intended to break the political deadlock between the Indian National Congress and the All-India Muslim League. The conference over which the Mission presided ended in failure. Wavell blamed Gandhi. He explained why in a letter to King George VI dated 8 July 1946

I can never entirely rid my mind of the recollection that in 1942, at almost the most critical period of the war for India, when I was endeavouring as Commander-in-Chief to secure India with very inadequate resources against Japanese invasion, the supporters of Congress made a deliberate effort to paralyse my communications to the Eastern Front by widespread sabotage and rioting.

I will not trouble Your Majesty with any details of the various phases of the ... [Cabinet Mission] negotiations; but I think that you may be interested in some estimate of the performance of the principal Indian personalities involved ...

Gandhi ran entirely true to form: his influence is still great; his line of thought and action at any given moment and on any particular issue is as unpredictable as ever; he never makes a prouncement that is not so qualified and so vaguely worded that it cannot be interpreted in whatever sense best suits him at a later stage; but however double-tongued he may be, he is quite single-minded on the one objective from which he has never swayed in the last 40 years, the elimination of the hated British influence from India. My distrust of this shrewd, malevolent [evil], old politician was deep before the Conference started; it is deeper than ever now.

MUSLIM OPPOSITION TO GANDHI

14. As expressed by Mohamed Ali Jinnah, the leader of the All-India Muslim League, in a statement to the press, 22 June 1942

I am glad that Gandhi has at last openly declared that unity and a Hindu–Muslim settlement can only come after the achievement of India's indpendence, and has thereby thrown off the cloak that he has worn for the last 22 years. He has tried to fool the Muslims but has at last shown himself in his true colours. I have held that Gandhi never wanted to settle the Hindu–Muslim question except on his own terms of Hindu domination. He alone has dashed our hopes whenever there was a chance of agreement ... It is clear to those who understand Gandhi's language that he wants the British Government to accept that Congress means India and that Gandhi means Congress, and to come to terms with him as the spokesman of all-India with regard to the transfer of power of government to a self-styled Indian National Congress ... so that Hindu Congress raj can dominate the Muslims and other minorities.

NOTE: Raj means rule or government. Hindu Congress raj means government by a Hindu Congress

GANDHI'S VISION OF INDIA'S FUTURE

15. In 1909, Gandhi wrote a pamphlet entitled 'Hind Swaraj' (Indian Home Rule or Self-Government). The pamphlet criticised modern industrial societies which had developed in the West. In Gandhi's eyes, these societies were based on greed, exploitation and materialism. He returned to this theme in a letter to Jawaharlal Nehru dated 5 October 1945

I have said that I fully stand by the kind of [government] which I have described in *Hind Swaraj* ... I believe that if India, and through India the world, is to achieve real freedom, then sooner or later we shall have to go and live in the villages – in huts, not in palaces. Millions of people can never live in cities and palaces in comfort and peace. Nor can they do so by killing one another, that is, by resorting to violence and untruth. I have not the slightest doubt that, but for the pair, truth and non-violence, mankind will be doomed. We can have the vision of that truth and non-violence only in the simplicity of the villages. That simplicity resides in the spinning wheel and what is implied by the spinning wheel ...

You will not be able to understand me if you think that I am talking about the villages of today. My ideal village still exists only in my imagination. In this village of my dreams the villager will not be dull – he will be all awareness. He will not live like an animal in filth and darkness. Men and women will live in freedom, prepared to face the whole world. There will be no plague, no cholera and no smallpox. Nobody will be allowed to be idle or to wallow in luxury. Everyone will have to do body [manual] labour. Granting all this I can still envisage a number of things that will have to be organised on a large scale. Perhaps there will even be railways and also post and telegraph offices. I do not know what things there will be or will not be. Nor am I bothered about it. If I can make sure of the essential thing, other things will follow in due course. But if I give up the essential thing, I give up everything.

16. Many of the Indian nationalists did not agree with Gandhi. Jawaharlal Nehru, India's first Prime Minister in 1947, replied to Gandhi in a letter dated 9 October 1945

I do not understand why a village should necessarily embody [represent] truth and non-violence. A village, normally speaking, is backward intellectually and culturally and no progress can be made from a backward environment. Narrow-minded people are much more likely to be untruthful and violent.

Then again we have to put down certain objectives like [sufficient] food, clothing, housing, education, sanitation etc., which should be the minimum requirement for the country and for everyone ... Again it seems to me inevitable that modern means of transport as well as many other modern developments must continue and be developed. There is no way out except to have them. If that is so inevitably a measure of heavy industry exists. How far will that fit in with a purely village society? ... I do not think it is possible for India to be really independent unless she is a technically advanced country. I am not thinking for the moment in terms of just armies but rather of scientific growth ... There is no question of palaces for millions of people. But there seem to be no reasons why millions should not have comfortable up-to-date homes where they can lead a cultured existence.

It is many years ago since I read *Hind Swaraj* and I have only a vague picture in my mind. But even when I read it 20 or more years ago it seemed to me completely unreal ... As you know, the Congress has never considered that picture, much less adopted it ... It is 38 years since *Hind Swaraj* was written. The world has completely changed since then ...

THE NATURE OF GANDHI'S APPEAL

17. W H Lewis, a British official in the province of Bihar, commenting on Gandhi's influence among the peasants in a district of the province, 29 April 1917

We may look upon Mr Gandhi as an idealist, a fanatic or a revolutionary according to our particular opinions. But to the *raiyats* [peasants] he is their liberator, and they credit him with extraordinary powers. He moves about in the villages, asking them to lay their grievances before him, and he is daily transfiguring [changing] the imaginations of masses of ignorant men with visions of an early millenium [a new age of happiness].

18. Subhas Chandra Bose was a Congress radical or left-winger and one of Gandhi's strongest critics. However, even the critics admitted that Gandhi had a unique appeal for the mass of the Indian people. In a book published in 1935, Bose had this to say about Gandhi's appeal

The role which a man plays in history depends partly on his physical and mental equipment – and partly on the environment and the needs of the time in which he is born. There is something in Mahatma Gandhi which appeals to the mass of the Indian people. Born in another country he might have been a complete misfit. What, for instance, would he have done in a country like Russia or Germany or Italy. His doctrine of non-violence would have led him to the cross or to the mental hospital. In India it is different. His simple life, his vegetarian diet, his goat's milk, his day of silence every week, his habit of squatting on the floor instead of sitting on a chair, his loincloth – in fact everything connected with him – has marked him out as one of the eccentric Mahatmas of old and has brought him nearer to his people. Wherever he may go, even the poorest of the poor feels that he is the product of the Indian soil – bone of his bone, flesh of his flesh. Whenever the Mahatma speaks, he does so in a language that they comprehend.

GANDHI'S RADICAL CRITICS

19. Gandhi was accused by his radical critics of wanting less than complete independence. They said that he was using his influence to prevent the growth of revolution in India. Shapurji Saklavata represented the constituency of Battersea in South London as a Labour MP in 1922 and as a Communist MP in 1924. He had this to say about Gandhi's Civil Disobedience movement in 1930

He [Gandhi] will never fight for India's freedom from the British yoke ... He is shrewd enough to know that complete independence for India will soon finish the power of the Indian princes and bourgeoisie and will end in a triumphant revolution of the workers and peasants. He is really shuddering at the thought of a Communist State: his ideal is a Dominion under British guns ... he cannot conceive of a great Indian Union of Soviets in which workers and peasants are supreme, and in which the princes and landlords, money-lenders and dividend earners, have no place at all ... As soon as Lord Irwin spoke of a smiling Round Table Conference of the thieves of the Empire, Gandhi rushed his country into it ... But immediately he found the young blood rising, and he still found the workers' and peasants' revolution growing. He thought it better to ride on the back of it than be crushed under it ...

Since then he has been shouting for a compromise, and by dramatic gestures he is striving to force a speedy compromise between the British and would-be Indian bourgeois leaders to stem the growth of proletarian [workers'] revolution ... He neglects the revolutionary side of the salt proposition. He does not call upon millions of Indian villagers to expel the special Salt Police from their villages and he does not call upon his own friends, the big Indian salt manufacturers, to refuse to pay the taxes and go to prison. He does not call upon his propertied [property-owning] and mill-owning friends to refuse to pay income tax and to go to prison. He does not support the railway strikers and textile strikers who were shot down, and his Congress Committee has not got a word of praise for the Indian troops at Peshawar [capital of the North-West Frontier Province] who practised true non-violence and refused to shoot down innocent people wanting their liberty from a foreign occupier of their country ...

Some people think that because Gandhi and some of his followers are put in prison ... and use strong words ... they will never again become friends of the British Empire. This is nonsense.

GANDHI'S INFLUENCE IN THE POST-WAR WORLD

20. *The views of Martin Luther King, the leader of the Black American Civil Rights campaign in the 1950s and 1960s*

The Gandhian concept [idea] of *satyagraha* was profoundly significant to me. As I delved [looked] deeper into the philosophy of Gandhi, my scepticism [doubts] concerning the power of love gradually diminished, and I came to see for the first time that the Christian doctrine of love, operating through the Gandhian method of non-violence, is one of the most potent [strongest] weapons available to an oppressed people in their struggle for freedom.

21. *Gandhi's influence in Africa, as expressed by Ali Mazrui, an African historian*

In Africa, the Gandhian torch passed to Kwame Nkrumah, the leader at that time of Gold Coast [Ghana] nationalism. In June 1949, Nkrumah launched his strategy of 'Positive Action' as a form of harassing the British authorities to grant one concession after another to the nationalist movement. In his autobiography Nkrumah tells how he explained the strategy to a critical traditional local council: 'I described Positive Action as the adoption of all legitimate and constitutional means by which we could attack the forces of imperialism in the country. The weapons were legitimate political agitation, newspaper and educational campaigns and, as a last resort, the constitutional application of strikes, boycotts and non-cooperation based on the principle of absolute non-violence as used by Gandhi in India.' With the launching of 'Positive Action', Nkrumah earned the name not only of 'Apostle of Freedom' but also of 'Gandhi of Ghana'. Years later, Nkrumah was to say, 'We salute Mahatma Gandhi and we remember in tribute to him, that it was in South Africa that this method of non-violence and non-cooperation was first practised.

CHAPTER NINE

THE GROWTH OF
MUSLIM SEPARATISM
AND THE PARTITION OF INDIA

The Muslims as India's largest minority community

The Indian Muslims were India's largest minority community. Of a total population of 294 million in 1901, more than a fifth – 62½ million – were Muslims. Muslims were scattered throughout the subcontinent but the majority lived in the regions of the north-west and north-east. In the north-west they were the descendants of powerful Muslim invaders from Central Asia. The invasions, which began in the eleventh century, paved the way for the Mughal empire in India. In the north-east, the Muslims were of humbler origin. The majority were poor cultivators, working land owned by Hindu landowners, and they were often converts from low caste Hindus.

The Muslims as a divided community

The Indian Muslims were no more a single and united community than were India's Hindus. They spoke different languages. They varied enormously in social and economic status. The Muslim aristocrat who lived in the United Provinces, the area which became the centre of Mughal power in India, had little in common with the poor Muslim peasant of East Bengal. In the late nineteenth century it was said that the Muslims were at a disadvantage when compared with the Hindus in terms of Western education. In the 1880s, Muslims represented 22 per cent of the total population but only 4 per cent of college students. The Hindus, by contrast, represented 73 per cent of the total population and 90 per cent of college students. However, these statistics do not tell the whole story. In Bengal, where Muslims were in a majority, the poor Muslim cultivator was no worse off than his low caste Hindu counterpart. Both were educationally deprived. But in the United Provinces, where Muslims were in a minority, upper-class Muslims enjoyed a standard of education which was equal to that of the Hindus.

The British view of the Muslims

The British tended to ignore the differences among Muslims. They also had their own explanation of why the Muslims were thought to be less successful in terms of education. The British viewed the Muslims as a distinct community, mainly because of their religion. Islam is based on belief in one supreme God. Muslims regard the Qur'an, their holy book, as the Word of God. It represents not only a set of beliefs but also a way of life. Islam was thought by the British to be the reason why the Muslims were reluctant to adapt to Western ideas in general and to Western education in particular. The British also believed that the Muslims in India clung to their own ways because of their political background. It was suggested that they were resentful because they had been replaced by the British as the rulers of India.

The Muslim image of themselves

The British therefore had an image of the Muslims as a distinct community with a proud past but with many disadvantages when compared with the Hindu majority. Although inaccurate in many ways, the image was a powerful one. It not only influenced the way in which the British saw the Muslims, but also the way in which many Muslims viewed themselves. How to maintain their own identity under foreign rule in a country in which they were in a minority was the main question which faced the Indian Muslims.

Syed Ahmed Khan and the Aligarh movement

The late nineteenth century answer to this question was provided by Syed Ahmed Khan. The author of *The Causes of the Indian Revolt* (see chapter 4, no 7), Syed Ahmed Khan argued that Muslims had to make good lost time by taking up Western education (No 1). For this purpose he planned a 'Muhammadan Anglo-Oriental College' where upper class Muslim boys would be taught in English. The college began as a primary school at Aligarh in the United Provinces in 1875. With the aid of a British grant and subscriptions from the Muslim aristocracy, the college soon became the centre of Muslim education in northern India. It was raised to the status of a university in 1921. Syed Ahmed Khan also believed that the Muslims could best defend their interests by proving that they were loyal to the British Government. He urged Muslims to keep out of politics and warned them against joining the Indian National Congress. He rejected the Congress claim that India was one nation and pointed out that the Muslims would be in danger if the British system of government was introduced into India (Nos 2–3).

The Muslim League and the separate Muslim electorate

Not all Muslims heeded Syed Ahmed Khan's warning. Between 1886 and 1905, some ten per cent of the delegates at the annual Congress meetings and two of the Congress Presidents were Muslim. But in 1906 the British Government announced its intention to reform the legislative councils. The councils were to be enlarged by electing more Indian members. For the government, the reforms were intended to rally the support of the moderates within the Indian National Congress and to isolate the extremists (see chapter 6). For a number of Muslims, however, the proposed reforms gave added weight to Sir Syed Ahmed Khan's warnings.

In October 1906 a deputation of thirty-five upper class Muslims had an audience with the Viceroy, Lord Minto. The members of the deputation argued that Western ideas of representative government were new to India. They suggested that Muslim represent-ation on the legislative councils should not be determined by their numbers alone. Account should also be taken of their historical and political importance as a distinct community. The Viceroy gave an encouraging reply. In December 1906 the first meeting of an All-India Muslim League was held at Dacca in East Bengal. The Muslim League was a departure from Syed Ahmed Khan's view that the Muslims should not engage in politics. However, the resolutions passed at the Dacca meeting confirmed that the Muslims were still loyal to the British Government. The reformed legislative councils were established under the Indian Councils Act of 1909. The Act introduced the principle of a separate Muslim electorate. In future, Muslim voters would elect Muslim candidates to fill a number of seats reserved for Muslims on the legislative councils. By this means the Muslims obtained greater parliamentary representation than their numbers alone would justify.

The separate electorate established the Muslims as a distinct political community. The Muslim League gave them their own political organisation. The part played by the British in these developments has always been controversial. Was British policy towards the Muslims based on the view that parliamentary government in the Western sense was unsuited to India because of the different communities and religions? Or were the British using the Muslims in a 'divide and rule' sense to weaken the nationalist movement in India which was led by the Hindu-dominated Indian National Congress? (Nos 4–10).

Dyarchy and the growth of communalism in India

The next major reform introduced by the British was the Government of India Act of 1919. The Act retained the separate electorate for Muslims. It also introduced the system of dyarchy in the provinces of British India. Dyarchy divided government in the provinces into reserved and transferred subjects. Reserved subjects covered the key areas of government, such as finance and taxation and law and order. These were left under the control of British Governors. Transferred subjects covered areas such as agriculture, education, public health, transport and local government. These areas were seen as nation-building activities. They became the responsibility of elected Indian ministers. Officially, the British claimed that dyarchy was the first in a series of reforms which would eventually lead to self-government in India. However, self-government was a long way off. In reality, dyarchy was seen by the British as a convenient way of maintaining their own interests in India. Indians were encouraged to involve themselves in the 'safe' areas of provincial government. The British were left in complete control of the central Government of India which was responsible for the whole country.

Under dyarchy in the 1920s, Indian politicians were able to make appointments to key jobs in the government of their provinces. They were also in a position to decide how money should be spent. In some provinces the politicians acted according to their class interests. For instance, landowning groups acted together. But in others the politicians acted upon the basis of their religious or caste interests. They allocated jobs and introduced new laws for the benefit of their own religious community or their own caste group. Dyarchy therefore had a tendency to emphasise the differences between the various religious and caste groups. Emphasising such differences was known as communalism.

Communalism led to competition and rivalry between different communities. It also led to conflict. In the 1920s there were a number of violent clashes between Hindus and Muslims. The issues of cow protection and the playing of music in front of mosques were often the causes. The activities of a number of communal organisations added to the tensions. The Arya Samaj was a Hindu communal body based in the Punjab. It organised the *shuddi* (purification) and *sangathan* (consolidation) movements with the aim of converting Muslims to Hinduism. In 1919 the *Hindu Mahasabha* (Great Assembly of Hindus) was formed to defend Hindus politically as well as religiously. The Muslims responded with the *tabligh* (education) and *tanzim* (organisation) movements. They were led by the *ulama* (the Muslim priesthood) with the aim of defending Islam and converting Hindus (Nos 11–13).

Muslim fears for their future and the idea of Pakistan

Muslim loyalty towards the British was undermined at the end of the First World War. Allied plans to break up the Turkish Empire persuaded a number of Muslims to join forces with Gandhi and Congress in the Khilafat and non-cooperation movements (see chapter 8). Both movements were shortlived. Gandhi suspended non-cooperation in 1922. The Khilafat movement began to lose ground in 1924 when a new revolutionary government in Turkey under the leadership of Kamal Pasha abolished the position of the Kalifah. Subsequent attempts to promote Hindu–Muslim unity met with little success. When the next round of political reforms was considered in the early 1930s, the Muslims had one major concern. The British had declared on more than one occasion that it was their intention to give self-government to India. They viewed self-government as a distant goal and refused to commit themselves to a date. But in the meantime the Muslims wanted safeguards. Looking to the future, the Muslims were determined that they should not be left under the control of the Hindu majority when India eventually became self-governing. To be both an Indian nationalist and a follower of Islam, posed a dilemma for the Muslims (No 14). Although at the time their ideas were not taken seriously, a number of Muslim writers in the early 1930s believed that the solution lay in the Muslims having a separate state of their own (No 15).

Mohamed Ali Jinnah and the revival of the Muslim League

For the first twenty-five years of its existence, the Muslim League was not an effective political party. Membership was low and it had little money. The League sprang to life in the late 1930s under the leadership of Mohamed Ali Jinnah. A lawyer by profession, Jinnah had been a member of Congress before the League was formed in 1906. When he joined the League he tried to use his influence to resolve the differences between Hindus and Muslims. It was a frustrating task and Jinnah became disillusioned. He gave up politics but was then persuaded out of retirement to lead the Muslim League in 1934. He set about rebuilding the League after its disastrous performance in the 1937 elections in the provinces of India. The League won less than a quarter of the seats reserved for Muslims. It was also defeated by provincial Muslim parties in Bengal and the Punjab, two provinces in which Muslims were the majority community. Insult was added to injury when the Congress leaders rejected League proposals for the formation of coalition governments elsewhere. The humiliation made Jinnah determined to force Congress to recognise the League as an equal. The Congress leaders had repeatedly claimed that

Congress was the only national party which represented all Indians, irrespective of their religion. Jinnah challenged this claim and set out to prove that the Muslim League alone represented India's Muslims (Nos 16–19). When it met at Lahore in March 1940, the League passed its famous 'Pakistan' resolution which called for the creation of independent Muslim 'states' in the north-western and north-eastern zones of India. Jinnah had now formed the opinion that Western-style democracy was unsuitable for India. In his speech at Lahore he declared that India represented not one, but two quite distinct and separate nations (No 20).

Direct Action Day

The Muslim League grew in strength during the Second World War. It had the political field to itself. Congress was outlawed and its leaders under arrest because of the Quit India movement. Elections in 1946 demonstrated that the League had overwhelming Muslim support. Negotiations between the League and Congress, with the British acting as a referee, broke down. A formula could not be found which would satisfy both the Congress demand for a united India and the League demand for effective Muslim safeguards. Pakistan was now defined as a single Muslim state. It would consist of the Muslim majority areas of the north-west and the north-east. The two halves of this new state would be separated by a thousand miles of Indian territory. As the deadlock continued, the struggle was carried to the streets. Violence between the rival communities increased. In August 1946, following the breakdown of important negotiations, Jinnah called for a Muslim day of 'Direct Action'. Intended as a day of peaceful protest, Direct Action resulted in over 4000 deaths in Calcutta alone (fig 9.1).

The partition of India

But just as Congress failed to achieve a united India, so Jinnah failed to achieve the Pakistan that he wanted. The logic of his argument was turned against him. If, as Jinnah insisted, India had to be divided, so too did the provinces that would be affected. Instead of a Pakistan which included the whole of Bengal and the Punjab, Jinnah had to be satisfied with what Lord Mountbatten, the last Viceroy, described as a 'moth-eaten' Pakistan (fig 9.2). The non-Muslim areas of Bengal and the Punjab remained with India. The boundary line in each province was decided by a Boundary Commission (fig 9.3). The Commission consisted of a British High Court Judge assisted by two Congress and two

TODAY IS——

DIRECT ACTION DAY

TODAY MUSLIMS OF INDIA DEDICATE ANEW THEIR LIVES AND ALL THEY POSSESS TO THE CAUSE OF FREEDOM

TODAY LET EVERY MUSLIM SWEAR IN THE NAME OF ALLAH TO RESIST AGGRESSION

DIRECT ACTION IS NOW THEIR ONLY COURSE

BECAUSE

- ★ They offered Peace but Peace was spurned
- ★ They honoured their word but were betrayed
- ★ They claimed Liberty but are offered Thraldom

NOW MIGHT ALONE CAN SECURE THEIR RIGHT

PAKISTAN IS OURS

- ★ BY RIGHT OF NATIONHOOD ★
- ★ BY RIGHT OF MAJORITY ★
- ★ BY RIGHT OF NATIONAL JUSTICE ★
- ★ BY RIGHT OF POPULAR VERDICT ★

WE SHALL FIGHT FOR IT . . . . . .
. . . . . . WE SHALL DIE FOR IT
TAKE IT WE MUST--OR PERISH

PLEDGE OF SACRIFICE

At The Convention Of National Legislators Held In Delhi On April 9-10, 1946, They Took The Following Pledge:

In the name of Allah, the Beneficent the Merciful

"Say: my prayer and my sacrifice and my living and my dying are all for Allah, the Lord of the Worlds" (Al-Quran)

I M. A. Jinnah, a member of the Muslim League Party of the ...... Central ...... Legislative ...... do hereby solemnly declare my firm conviction that the safety and security, and the salvation and destiny of the Muslim nation inhabiting the sub-continent of India lie only in the achievement of Pakistan which is the one equitable, honourable and just solution of the constitutional problem and which will bring peace, freedom and prosperity to the various nationalities and communities of this great sub-continent.

I most solemnly affirm that I shall willingly and unflinchingly carry out all the directions and instructions which may be issued by the All-India Muslim League in pursuance of any movement launched by it for the attainment of the cherished national goal of Pakistan, and, believing as I do in the righteous and the justice of my cause, I pledge myself to undergo any danger, trial or sacrifice which may be demanded of me.

"Our Lord! Bestow on us endurance, and keep our steps firm and help us against the disbelieving people." Amen!

Signature M.A.Jinnah

Dated 9th April 1946

TODAY LET EVERY MUSLIM ALSO TAKE THIS PLEDGE OF SACRIFICE IN THE CAUSE OF NATIONAL FREEDOM

THE RESOLUTION

THE FOLLOWING IS THE FULL TEXT OF THE DIRECT ACTION RESOLUTION PASSED UNANIMOUSLY BY THE MUSLIM NATIONAL PARLIAMENT, IN BOMBAY, ON JULY 29, 1946:

"Whereas the All-India Muslim League has today resolved to reject the proposals embodied in the statement of the Cabinet Delegation and the Viceroy dated May 16. 1946. due to the intransigence of the Congress on the one hand and the breach of faith with the Muslims by the British Government on the other;

"And whereas Muslim India has exhausted without success all efforts to find a peaceful solution of the Indian problem by compromise and constitutional means; and whereas the Congress is bent upon setting up a caste-Hindu Raj in India with the connivance of the British; and whereas recent events have shown that power politics and not justice and fairplay are deciding factors in Indian affairs;

Achievement Of Pakistan

"And whereas it has become abundantly clear that the Muslims of India would not rest content with anything less than the immediate establishment of an Independent and full Sovereign State of Pakistan and would resist any attempt to impose any constitution, long-term or short-term, or setting up of any Interim Government at the Centre without the approval and consent of the Muslim League, the Council of the All-India Muslim League is convinced that now the time has come for the Muslim Nation to resort to Direct Action to achieve Pakistan and to get rid of the present slavery under the British and contemplated future caste-Hindu domination."

Be Ready For Every Sacrifice

"This Council calls upon the Muslim Nation to stand to a man behind their sole representative organisation—the All-India Muslim League—and be ready for every sacrifice.

"This Council directs the Working Committee to prepare forthwith a programme of Direct Action to carry out the policy initiated above and to organise the Muslims for the coming struggle to be launched as and when necessary.

"As a protest against and in token of their deep resentment of the attitude of the British, this Council calls upon the Musalmans to renounce forthwith the titles conferred upon them by the Alien Government."

IT IS NOW FOR THE NATION TO CARRY IT OUT

9.1 The Muslim League's 'Direct Action Day', 16 August 1946. An advertisement which appeared in Dawn, an English-language newspaper started by Jinnah in 1941 to represent the views of the Muslim League.

Muslim League judges. The boundary line in the Punjab angered the more militant Sikhs. It cut through the Sikh homeland and the militants threatened violence. When the decisions of the Boundary Commission were announced the day after independence in August 1947, the violence exploded. Estimates of the numbers killed in the Punjab in the weeks which followed varied from 200,000 to more than one million. Over eleven million people became refugees (No 21).

Jinnah's influence

Mohamed Ali Jinnah has always been a controversial figure (Nos 22–26). Pakistan's first Governor-General when British rule ended in August 1947, Jinnah died in September 1948. In an age sceptical of the role of 'great men' in history, there are still those who believe that Jinnah alone brought Pakistan into being. To this day he is revered in Pakistan as *Quaid-i-Azam* – The Great Leader.

THE VIEWS OF SYED AHMED KHAN

1. On Western education

It is not only because the British are today our rulers, and we have to recognise this fact if we are to survive, that I am advocating the adoption of their system of education, but also because Europe has made such remarkable progress in science that it would be suicidal not to make an effort to acquire it. Already the leeway [gap] between our knowledge and that of Europe is too great. If we go on with our present obstinacy in neglecting it, we shall be left far behind. How can we remain true Muslims or serve Islam, if we sink into ignorance?

2. On the Indian National Congress

The aims and objects of the Indian National Congress are based upon an ignorance of history and present-day realities; they do not take into consideration that India is inhabited by different nationalities; they presuppose that the Muslims, the Marathas, the Brahmins, the Kshatriyas, the Banias, the Sudras, the Sikhs, the Bengalis, the Madrasis, and the Peshawaris can all be treated alike and all of them belong to the same nation. The Congress thinks that they profess the same religion, that they speak the same language, that their way of life and customs are the same, that their attitude to History is similar and is based on the same historical traditions ... For the successful

9.2 *A Hindu view of the Muslim League's demand for Pakistan, from the* Tribune, *a pro-Indian National Congress Indian newspaper, 15 April 1946. Jinnah is portrayed as the figure holding the paintbrush.*

running of a democratic government it is essential that the majority should have the ability to govern not only themselves but also unwilling minorities ... I consider the experiment which the Indian National Congress wants to make fraught with dangers and suffering for all the nationalities of India, especially for the Muslims.

3. On democratic government

The second demand of the National Congress is that the people should elect a section of the Viceroy's Council ... Now, let us suppose the Viceroy's Council made in this manner. And let us suppose first of all that we have universal suffrage [one person, one vote], as in America, and that that everybody, *chamars* [shoemakers] and all, have votes. And first suppose that all the Mahomedan electors vote for a Mahomedan member and all Hindu electors for a Hindu member, and now count how many votes the Mahomedan member has and how many the Hindu. It is certain that the Hindu member will have four times as many because their population is four times as numerous. Therefore we can prove by mathematics that there will be four votes for the Hindu to every one vote for the Mahomedan. And now how can the Mahomedan guard his interests? It would be like a game of dice, in which one man had four dice and the other only one. In the second place, suppose that the electorate be limited. Some method of qualification must be made; for example, that people with a certain income shall be electors. Now, I ask you, O Mahomedans! Weep at your condition! Have you such wealth that you can compete with the Hindus? ... In the normal case no single Mahomedan will secure a seat in the Viceroy's Council ...

DIVIDE AND RULE?

4. Lord Dufferin (Viceroy 1884–88), in a letter to the editor of the Pioneer newspaper, 1 January 1887

The diversity of races in India and the presence of a powerful Mahomedan community, are undoubtedly circumstances favourable to the maintenance of our rule; but these circumstances we found and did not create, nor, had they been non-existent, would we have been justified in establishing them by artificial means. It would be a diabolical policy on the part of any Government to endeavour to exacerbate [aggravate] race hatreds among the Queen's Indian subjects for a political object.

5. The idea that a Muslim deputation should have an audience with the Viceroy, Lord Minto, originated in August 1906 in a letter from Mohsin ul-Mulk, the secretary of the Aligarh college, to the college principal, Mr Archibold. The letter referred to a speech by John Morley, the Secretary of State for India, which announced the Government's intention to reform the legislative councils in India

You must have read and thought over Mr John Morley's speech ... It is very much talked of among Mahommedans of India and is commonly believed to be a great success achieved by the [Indian] National Congress. You are aware that the Mohammedans already feel a little disappointed, and young educated Mohammedans seem to have a sympathy for the 'Congress' and this speech will probably produce a greater tendency in them to join the Congress ... I have several letters drawing attention to the new proposal of 'elected representatives' in the Legislative Councils. They say that the existing rules confer no rights on Mohammedans; and no Mohammedans get

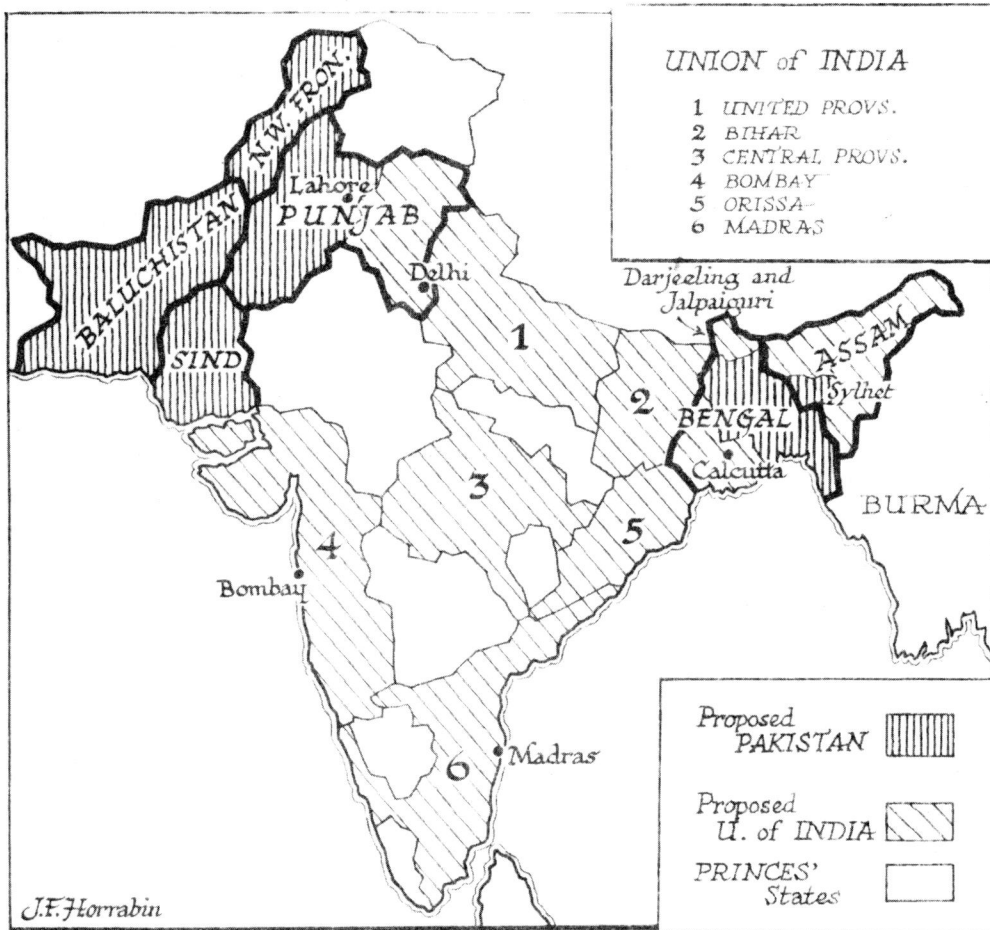

9.3 *The Partition of India, 1947.*

into the Councils by election ... If the new rules now to be drawn up introduce 'election' on a more extended scale, the Mohammedans will hardly get a seat and no Mohammedans will get into the Councils by election.

6. *Lord Minto to John Morley, 8 August 1906*

I think it is worthwhile to enclose you a copy of a letter to Mr Archibold ... from

Mohsin ul-Mulk ... It was only put before me today and is important as illustrating the trend of Mohammedan thought, and the apprehension that Mohammedan interests may be neglected in dealing with any increase of representation on the legislative councils. There have been other signs ... pointing in the same direction, and there is no doubt a natural fear in many quarters lest perpetual Bengalee demands should lead to the neglect of other claims to representation throughout India; so that we must be very careful in taking up these questions to give full value to the importance of other interests besides those so largely represented by the Congress.

7. Sir Denzil Ibbetson, Lieutenant-Governor of the Punjab, in a letter to Mr Dunlop Smith, Lord Minto's Private Secretary, 10 August 1906

I have heard from other quarters also what Mohsin ul-Mulk says about the aspirations of the younger generation of Mohammedans. Their aspirations are perfectly natural. But it would be a calamity if they were to drive those who feel them into the arms of the Congress party; for at present the educated Mohammedan is the most conservative element in Indian society.

8. Lord Minto's reply to the Muslim deputation, October 1906

You need not ask my pardon, gentlemen, for telling me that 'representative institutions of the European type are entirely new to the people of India', or that their introduction here requires the most earnest thought and care. I should be very far from welcoming all the political machinery of the Western world amongst the hereditary instincts and traditions of Eastern races ... I am as firmly convinced, as I believe you to be, that any electoral representation in India would be doomed to mischievous failure which aimed at granting a personal enfranchisement [voting rights] regardless of the beliefs and traditions of the communities composing the population of this Continent. The great mass of the people of India have no knowledge of representative institutions. In the meantime I can only say to you that the Mohammedan community may rest assured that their political rights and interests as a community will be safeguarded in any administrative reorganisation with which I am concerned ...

9. Lord Minto to Sir Arthur Godley on the value of the Muslim deputation, 17 October 1906

I entirely agree with you as to the value of the recent Mohammedan demonstrations. They have been most fortunate and have really done much to save the position, for, as you say, they will be a useful reminder to the people in England that the Bengali is not everybody in India, in fact the Mohammedan Community, when roused, would be a much stronger and more dangerous factor to deal with than the Bengalis.

10. *The aims of the Muslim League, as defined in 1912*

(1) To promote and maintain among Indians feelings of loyalty towards the British Crown; (2) To protect and advance the political and other rights and interests of the Indian Musalmans; (3) To promote friendship and union between the Musalmans and other communities of India; and (4) Without detriment [harm] to the foregoing objects, the attainment of a system of self-government suitable to India ...

THE GROWTH OF COMMUNALISM IN INDIA

11. *Extract from the Report of the Indian Statutory Commission, 1930. The Commission was appointed in 1927 to review the working of the 1919 Government of India Act*

It unfortunately happens that on Indian soil the opposition of these two faiths is sharply intensified by religious practices which are only too likely to provoke mutual ill-feeling. The devout Hindu regards the cow as an object of great veneration [respect], while the ceremonial sacrifice of cows or other animals is a feature of the annual Muhammadan festival known as the *Baqr'Id*. Hindu music played through the streets on the occasion of the procession of an idol, or in connection with a marriage celebration, may take place at a time when the Muhammadans of the town are at worship in an adjoining mosque, and hence arises an outbreak of resentment which is apt to degenerate into a serious quarrel. The religious anniversaries observed by Muslims are fixed by reference to a lunar year which does not correspond with the adjusted Hindu calendar, and consequently it occasionally happens that dates of special importance in the two religions coincide – as, for instance, when an anniversary of Moslem mourning synchronises with a day of Hindu rejoicing – and the authorities responsible for the maintenance of law and order are then faced with a time of special anxiety. Inspite of the constant watchfulness of the police authorities, and of the earnest efforts of leaders in both communities to reach a *modus vivendi* [working arrangement], the immediate occasion of communal disorder is nearly always the religious issue. On the other hand, when communal feeling is roused on some matter of secular [non-religious] interest, religious zeal [fanaticism] is always present to stimulate conflict, and partisans are not slow to exploit the opportunity.

12. *In 1931, during the civil disobedience movement in India, Hindu–Muslim riots broke out at Cawnpore in the United Provinces. A Commission of Enquiry was appointed to determine the causes. The following is an extract from the evidence of Brij Narain Miroutra, a Hindu lawyer and a resident of Cawnpore, 30 April 1931*

When Mahatma Gandhi launched his movement of Civil Disobedience the Hindus of

Cawnpore, with rare exceptions, either took an active part in the movement or fully sympathised with it. While the Hindu cloth dealers were picketed so that not an inch of foreign cloth should escape, the Mohammedan shops were not picketed, because the Mohammedans as a class were opposed to the movement and showed fight ... The Mohammedans of Cawnpore are communalists and did not approve of the Civil Disobedience movement. The movement was considered by them to be a purely Hindu movement ... From the beginning of August 1930 it became obvious that the Mohammedans were organising themselves ... They formed processions with green flags, big and small, of silk and gold and silver threads, on big poles, *lathi*s and *danda*s [clubs and sticks]. Some again wore military uniforms. They were joined by bands of Kabulis. Some of these processions were taken out on Sundays to enable mill hands to join them. They were accompanied by cries of *Allah-o-Akbar* [God is Great, the Muslim battle cry] and *Shaukat Ali Zindabad* [Long live Shaukat Ali, a Muslim leader] and offensive slogans and songs such as: '*Charkh hila denge kafir ko mita denge*' [We will move the universe and we will annihilate the infidels].

13. The Cawnpore riots. Evidence of Hafiz Mohammed Hussain, a Muslim shoe merchant and a resident of Cawnpore, 2 May 1931. The witness refers to Bhagat Singh, a Hindu revolutionary convicted on a charge of a terrorist murder and executed by the British in 1931. It also referes to the Gandhi–Irwin Pact of March 1931 as a result of which the civil disobedience movement was suspended temporarily

The immediate causes of the outbreak are traceable to the forcible closing of shops by the working agents of the Cawnpore Congress Working Committee. A good deal of unbearable pressure was brought to bear upon the Muslims to close their shops, as also upon the passers-by who were called upon to leave their conveyances [means of transport] and to walk on foot bareheaded as a mark of respect to the departed Bhagat Singh and his associates ... [T]he Muslims consider themselves to be let down by the British Government since the introduction of the reforms of 1919. The Hindus have since become elated and prone to carry out things in an upperhand manner owing to their being in a majority. The feelings ran very high between Hindus and Muslims since the Irwin–Gandhi Pact, which has helped to aggravate matters. The Hindus were thereby lead to believe and to presume that the *Swaraj* or responsible self-government will be acquired by them in no time and that the community in the minority must remain in complete subjugation to that in the majority. To assert their superiority the Congress people of Cawnpore made a common cause in the matter of taking up offensives against the Cawnpore Muslims without any provocation on the part of the latter, they being taken quite unawares and not being prepared at all for for the onslaught made upon them all of a sudden. A great influx of outsiders took place during the riot, lending a helping hand to the blood-thirsty persons in the very act of slaughtering Muslims; women and children having not been excepted. It is an established and undisputed fact that more Muslims than Hindus have been killed.

THE MUSLIM DILEMMA AND THE IDEA OF A SEPARATE MUSLIM STATE

14. Speech by Muhammad Ali (not to be confused with Mohamed Ali Jinnah, the leader of the Muslim League), at the Round Table Conference in London in 1930

Where God commands ... I am a Muslim first, a Muslim second and a Muslim last and nothing but a Muslim ...My first duty is to my Maker ... But where India is concerned, where India's freedom is concerned, where the welfare of India is concerned, I am an Indian first, an Indian second, an Indian last and nothing but an Indian. I belong to two circles of equal size but which are not concentric [having a common centre]. One is India and the other is the Muslim world ... we belong to these circles ... and we can leave neither.

15. Muhammad Iqbal, a poet-philosopher from the Punjab, was one of the first Muslims to suggest the idea a separate Muslim state. The following is an extract from his presidential address at a meeting of the Muslim League in December 1930

The units of India are not territorial as in European countries. India is a continent of human groups belonging to different races, speaking different languages and professing different religions. Their behaviour is not at all determined by race consciousness. Even the Hindus do not form a homogeneous group. The principle of European democracy cannot be applied to India without recognizing the fact of communal groups. The Muslim demand for the creation of a Muslim India within India is, therefore, perfectly justified ... Personally, I would go further ... I would like to see the Punjab, North-West Frontier Province, Sind and Baluchistan amalgamated into a single State. Self-government within the British empire or without the British empire, the formation of a consolidated North-West Indian Muslim State appears to me to be the final destiny of the Muslims, at least of North-West India.

NOTE: The name Pakistan is formed from the letters of the areas mentioned by Iqbal together with Kashmir: P for the Punjab, A for Afghania (the North-West Frontier Province), K for Kashmir, S for Sind and TAN for BaluchisTAN

THE DEVELOPMENT OF THE MUSLIM LEAGUE

16. *Speech by Jinnah as President of the Muslim League, December 1938*

As I have said before, there are four forces at play in this country. Firstly, there is the British Government. Secondly, there are the rulers and peoples of the Indian States. Thirdly, there are the Hindus; and fourthly, there are Muslims. The Congress press may clamour [protest] as much as it likes; they may bring out their morning, afternoon, evening and night editions; the Congress leaders may shout as much as they like that the Congress is a national body. But I say it is not true. The Congress is nothing but a Hindu body. That is the truth and the Congress leaders know it. The presence of the few Muslims, the few and misguided ones, and the few who are there with ulterior motives, does not, and cannot, make it a national body. I challenge anybody to deny that the Congress is not mainly a Hindu body. I ask, does the Congress represent the Muslims? (Shouts of 'No, no' which were repeated as indicated below.)

I ask does the Congress represent the Christians? ('No.')

I ask does the Congress represent the Scheduled Castes? ('No.')

I ask does the Congress represent the non-Brahmans? ('No.')

17. *Between 1937 and the outbreak of the war in 1939 Congress Governments held office in the Hindu-majority provinces of India. The Muslim League alleged that these governments discriminated against the Muslim minorities of the Hindu-majority provinces. The League published reports outlining Muslim grievances. Two specific grievances were summarised in this letter, dated 22 December 1939, from a district Muslim League in Bombay to the Governor, Sir Roger Lumley*

The Congress Government, both in the discharge of its duties of administration and in the Legislature, has done its best to flout [express contempt for] Muslim opinion and destroy Muslim culture and has interfered with their religious and social life and trampled upon their economic and political rights.

1. The tricolour flag is the flag of the Congress, a political party in India. It is in no way a National flag. Muslims owe no allegiance to it. The Congress persists in calling it the National flag, in spite of the fact that all other political parties have repeatedly repudiated [rejected] that claim of the Congress. Under these circumstances, the Congress is not at all justified in hoisting the tricolour Congress flag over public buildings in which Muslims, other minorities and political parties other than the Congress have as much right and interest as the Congress ...

2. With a view to suppress Islamic culture and diffuse [spread] Hindu ideology which is the very opposite of the basic principles of Islam, the Congress Government made particular efforts to introduce the idolatrous and anti-Muslim song of *Bande*

Mataram as a National song, in spite of united and strong opposition. Further, with a view to extort [force] respect for the same, the Congress Ministry issued orders to the effect that all government servants should stand up when it was sung. This compelled Muslims in the Government service to stand up even against their conscience. The said orders are in force even today and Your Excellency is requested to set them aside as early as possible.

18. Muslim grievances became the subject of an exchange of letters between Nehru and Jinnah in 1938. In these extracts from his letter to Jinnah, dated 6 April 1938, Nehru replied to Muslim allegations concerning the Bande Mataram song and the Congress flag. He also commented on the Muslim League's claim to be the only organisation representing India's Muslims

First of all, it has to be remembered that no formal national anthem has been adopted by the Congress at any time. It is true, however, that the *Bande Mataram* song has been intimately [closely] associated with Indian nationalism for more than thirty years ... Popular songs are not made to order, nor can they be successfully imposed. They grow out of public sentiment. During all these thirty or more years the *Bande Mataram* song was treated as a national song in praise of India ... When, however, some objections were raised, the [Congress] Working Committee carefully considered the matter and ultimately decided to recommend that certain stanzas [verses] ... might not ɔe used on national platforms or occasions ... But to compel large numbers of people to give up what they have long valued and grown attached to is to cause needless hurt to them and to injure the national movement itself ...

Obviously, a country and a national movement must have a national flag representing the nation and all communities in it. No communal flag can represent the nation. If we did not have a national flag now we would have to evolve one. The present national flag had its colours originally selected in order to represent the various communities, but we did not like to lay stress on this communal aspect of the colours. Artistically, I think the combination of orange, white and green has resulted in a flag which is probably the most beautiful of all national flags ... It is difficult to understand how anyone can reasonably object to it now. Communal flags cannot obviously take its place for that can only mean a host of flags of various communities being used together and thus emphasising our disunity and separateness. Communal flags might be used for religious functions, but they have no place at any national functions or over any public buildings meant for various communities ...

I do not understand what is meant by our recognition of the Muslim League as the one and only organisation of Indian Muslims. Obviously the Muslim League is an important communal organisation and we deal with it as such. But we have to deal with all organisations and individuals that come within our ken [range of vision]. We do not determine the measure of importance or distinction they possess … Inevitably the more important the organisation the more attention paid to it, but this importance does not come from outside recognition, but from inherent strength …

19. Jinnah's reply to Nehru, 12 April 1938

Your tone and language again display the same arrogance and militant spirit, as if the Congress is the sovereign [ruling] power … Here I add that in my opinion, unless the Congress recognises the Muslim League on a footing of complete equality and is prepared as such to negotiate for a Hindu–Muslim settlement, we shall have to wait and depend upon our inherent strength which will 'determine the measure of importance and distinction it possesses'. Having regard to your mentality, it is really rather difficult for me to make you understand the position any further.

THE PAKISTAN RESOLUTION OF 1940

20. Jinnah's speech in support of the resolution at the Lahore meeting of the Muslim League, March 1940

The Hindus and Muslims belong to two different religious philosophies, social customs, literatures. They neither intermarry nor interdine together and, indeed, they belong to two different civilisations which are based mainly on conflicting ideas and conceptions. Their outlooks on life and of life are different. It is quite clear that Hindus and Musulmans derive their inspiration from different sources of history. They have different epics, different heroes, and different episodes. Very often the hero of one is a foe of the other and, likewise, their victories and defeats overlap. To yoke [join] together two such nations under a single state, one as a numerical minority and the other as a majority, must lead to growing discontent and final destruction of any fabric that may be so built up for the government of such a state.

THE PARTITION OF INDIA

21. Note on the Punjab by Field Marshal Sir Claude Auchinleck, the last British Commander-in-Chief of the Indian Army. Auchinleck wrote this note on Independence day, 15 August 1947. The note described a situation which had become more serious in the weeks leading up to independence. It therefore warned of what was likely to happen in the Punjab on a much larger scale when the decisions of the Boundary Commission were announced

Amritsar and vicinity. The strife here was started by the Sikhs who have formed armed bands of considerable strength which are carrying out raids on Muslim or preponder-antly Muslim villages. Three or four of such raids have been occurring nightly. These bands are well organised and often include mounted men who are used as scouts to reconnoitre for a favourable opportunity. One such band is reliably reported to have killed 200 Muslims in one village a few days ago. The connivance of subjects of Sikh states is strongly suspected. There are also Muslim bands organised for the same purpose, but these are fewer in number, smaller in size and less well organised apparently ... In Amritsar City the casualties (predominantly Muslim apparently) were high and largely due to the emasculation [weakening] of the City Police force by the disarming by a new Superintendent of Police of the Muslim members of it. This has since been rectified and the official replaced. Several houses were burning in Amritsar City as I flew over it and four or five villages within ten or fifteen miles of the City were apparently completely destroyed by fire and still burning. The army is occupying the City in some strength.

Lahore. The aggression here is chiefly by Muslims, said to be in retaliation for the massacring of Muslims in Amritsar. The most disturbing feature here is the defection of the Police, particularly the special Police, who are predominantly Muslim. There is very strong evidence that the Police are taking little notice of the orders of their officers (all the remaining European officers left yesterday) and that they have actually joined hands with the rioters in certain instances. But for the presence of the Army there would now be a complete holocaust in the City ... It is estimated that as many as one tenth of the houses in Lahore City may have been destroyed by fire, or say 15% of the total area of the City. Destruction to this extent was not readily apparent as I flew over the City but shells of burnt out houses are not always easy to distinguish in a crowded city like Lahore. A large number of houses were still burning and a thick pall [dark cloak] of smoke hung over the City. There were also many houses on fire in the neighbouring suburbs and villages. The roads and streets were practically deserted.

DIFFERENT VIEWS OF MOHAMED ALI JINNAH

22. *Jawaharlal Nehru, as reported in an interview with Lord Mountbatten, the last Viceroy, 24 March 1947*

I asked him [Nehru] about Mr Jinnah. He gave me a remarkable word-picture of Jinnah's character. He described him as one of the most extraordinary men in history. A financially successful though mediocre lawyer, Jinnah had found success late in life. He had not been politically successful until after the age of 60. Nehru explained

Jinnah's creed, which he admitted had scored enormous success, as always to avoid taking positive action which might split his followers; to refuse to hold meetings or to answer questions; never to make a progressive statement because it might lead to internal Muslim dissensions. These negative qualities were ones which had a direct appeal to the Muslims.

23. Lord Mountbatten. The last Viceroy had regular staff meetings with his senior policy advisers. The following is an extract from the record of the meeting held on 11 April 1947

HIS EXCELLENCY THE VICEROY said that it had always been and would remain his desire to hand over power to a unified India ... He had now had six meetings with Mr Jinnah. The one the previous day had lasted for three hours. He had brought all possible arguments to bear on Mr Jinnah but it seemed that appeals to his reason did not prevail. He had pointed out to Mr Jinnah the enormous advantages of retaining a unified India – as one India could be immensely powerful and in the front rank of world powers. Mr Jinnah had not been able in his presence to adduce [put forward] one single feasible argument in favour of Pakistan. In fact he had offered no counter arguments. He gave the impression that he was not listening. He was impossible to argue with ... Mr Jinnah was a psychopathic case ... He [the Viceroy] added that until he had met Mr Jinnah he had not thought it possible that a man with such a complete lack of a sense of responsibility could hold the power which he did.

24. Z H Zaidi, a Pakistani historian. In making the following comments, Zaidi pointed out that from 1938 until his death in 1948, Jinnah fought against prolonged bouts of illness. He suffered from tuberculosis but his illness remained a closely guarded secret

How could the autocratic, cold, calculating figure of popular myth have attracted the loyalty and affection of so many prominent and experienced politicians, and of countless party workers? It was not as a dictator that he exercised power, but as a man able to charm friends and enemies alike into compliance. When he replied to almost every letter sent to him, it does not so much display his famous efficiency and legal-minded concern for detail but rather his concern for those whose leader he was ... [A]n enormous burden was placed upon Jinnah's strength and health by the weight of correspondence with which he had to deal. He always willingly shouldered that burden – even insisting on personally signing every Muslim Leaguer's subscription receipt: that was one of the ways in which he emphasised and cemented bonds between himself and his supporters, one of the penalties of leadership.

IN RETROSPECT

25. *B R Nanda, an Indian historian*

No serious attempt at a compromise solution could, however, be made. From 1937 to 1940, Jinnah refused to start a dialogue with the Congress until it conceded the League's right to be the exclusive representative of the Muslim community. From 1940 onwards, he refused to start a dialogue until the Congress conceded the principle of the partition of India. He did not elaborate the constitutional, economic and even geographic content of his proposal. While the Congress attitude towards the constitutional future of India underwent important changes between 1939 and 1946, Jinnah did not meet the Congress half-way, not even quarter-way. He did not budge an inch from the position he adopted. Every overture was rejected; every concession treated as a bargaining counter for a better deal. Only once, in June 1946, he seemed to agree to a compromise by accepting the cabinet mission plan; but his acceptance ... was more apparent than real; in any case it was withdrawn within seven weeks.

26. *M A H Ispahani, a member of the Muslim League Working Committee until 1947 and after independence a Pakistini diplomat*

The trouble with the Hindu leaders was that they lived in a world of make-believe and adopted an arrogant and domineering attitude towards the Muslims, as if the latter were a subject race who should live at the sufferance of the Hindu majority. They did not correctly guage the Muslim mind and always miscalculated the strength of Muslim feeling and determination ... [T]he Hindu leaders always started by opposing even the moderate demands of the Muslims. By the time they came round to recognize these demands, the Muslims had moved a step forward. The Congress contemptuously rejected Jinnah's modest proposals in 1928, spurned his offer of co-operation in 1937 and 1939 and sabotaged the compromise plan for a united India in 1946, but after each stage and every refusal and every rejection it had to yield more ground ... Even when they agreed to partition, the Congress did so with mental reservations, feeling confident that Pakistan would prove unworkable and would eventually be absorbed into India.

CHAPTER TEN

THE TRANSFER OF POWER

The significance of the Transfer of Power

As long as we rule India, we are the greatest power in the world. If we lose it, we shall drop straight away to a third-rate power.

So wrote Lord Curzon, Viceroy of India, in 1901. In August 1947 the unthinkable for Curzon happened. Britain handed over power to a new Government of India and to the Government of a new Muslim state of Pakistan. The ending of British rule in India was one of the most important events of the twentieth century. In India, it created the world's largest parliamentary democracy. In Pakistan, until the civil war and the emergence of Bangladesh in 1971, it created the world's largest (in terms of population) Muslim state. But it also had consequences which extended far beyond the Indian subcontinent. It was the first time in Asia that a European power had given up part of its empire and it set a pattern for the future. European colonial empires, French and Dutch as well as British, began to retreat under pressure from a new wave of Asian nationalism.

Historians have suggested three reasons to explain how and why India and Pakistan became independent in 1947. First, the strength of Indian nationalism; secondly, the changing nature of Britain's interests in India; and, finally, the effects on both India and Britain of the Second World War. This chapter examines the significance of each in turn.

Indian Nationalism

Unlike the nationalists in French Indo-China and Dutch Indonesia, the Indian nationalists did not have to fight a long and bitter anti-colonial war to gain their freedom. Instead they relied, in the main, on non-violent methods of political protest. The British met this protest with repression on the one hand but with reform on the other. A mere few thousand amidst a population of nearly 400 million, the British had never ruled India entirely on their own. They always depended on Indian support and cooperation. To obtain this support the British had to introduce political reforms. They also had to appoint more Indian officers in the Indian army and to increase the numbers of Indians serving in the civil services. From the 1930s, it became more difficult to attract British recruits to the Indian Civil Service. A career in India no longer offered long-term job security. In the provinces of India, political reforms meant giving more power to Indian politicians. The prospect of serving under Indian ministers was not one that appealed to many British civil servants. By the end of the Second World War, the British faced a serious manpower shortage. There were less than 500 senior British civil servants and only 200 police in the whole of India. Those who remained worked under increasingly difficult conditions and morale was low. In short, by 1947, the British no longer had the means to govern India effectively. Indians were virtually running their own country (Nos 1–2). Nationalism played a crucial role in these developments. Had it not been for the determination of the nationalist leaders that the British should leave India, British rule would certainly have been smoother and might well have lasted longer.

The Changing Nature of Britain's Interests in India

A second explanation suggests that where once Britain's interests in India made British rule absolutely vital, this was perhaps no longer the case by the 1930s and 1940s. At the height of British power at the turn of the century, Britain had governed India in order to acquire maximum profit at minimum expense. Questions of prestige apart, India had been important to Britain for two reasons. First, she was an important source for raw materials and a major market for cotton manufactures, especially cotton textiles. Secondly, she provided Britain with enormous military resources (see chapter 5). The Indian army, the largest volunteer army anywhere in the world, provided the means whereby the British Empire could expand and defend its influence from the Middle East to the Pacific. In 1882 Lord Salisbury likened India to 'an English barrack in the Oriental Seas from which we may draw any number of troops without paying for them' (fig 10.1).

British Trade with India

But from the end of the First World War, the pattern of Britain's relationship with India began to change. India was still an important market for British goods but no longer a vital one. Britain's export trade declined during the inter-war years. So too did the percentage of that trade which was exported to India. The older and more traditional British industries – such as textiles, shipbuilding, coal, and iron and steel – had been geared to exports. But they now carried less weight in the British economy. Their share of overseas markets began to dwindle in the face of foreign competition. They were also hit by the depression of the early 1930s and the world-wide trend away from free trade towards protection. To protect their own industries, a number of countries imposed customs duties on foreign imports. The 'new' industries which were emerging in Britain – in motor vehicles, chemicals, electrical goods and engineering – relied far less on overseas markets. These new industries found little outlet for their goods in India, nor did they depend on India for raw materials (No 3). To the extent that British trade with India was still important, direct political control was no longer essential. Trading links could be established with the independent governments of India and Pakistan. Private British business interests within India, particularly in tea and jute, could be protected in the same way.

On top of this, political changes in India made it difficult to maintain British trade on the same privileged terms. To finance the dyarchy reforms introduced under the 1919 Government of India Act (see chapter 9), the provinces of India had to be given their own sources of income. But giving money to the provinces meant taking it away from the central Government of India. To make good its losses, the Government of India had two options. It could either raise income tax or raise customs tariffs. The first would be unpopular in India. The second would be unpopular in Britain, particularly with the mill-owners of Lancashire. In the late nineteenth century British opinion had counted for more than Indian opinion. But now the position had changed. The Government of India could not afford to offend Indian opinion because it needed Indian cooperation to work the dyarchy reforms. It therefore chose the second option of raising customs tariffs. The Lancashire cotton interest suffered. The mill owners protested but to no avail. In 1926 the excise duty on Indian cotton goods, which had aroused such resentment in India when it was introduced in 1894, was abolished. Increasingly, the political situation in India made it difficult for the Government in London to dictate the financial policy of the Government of India (No 4).

10.1 'An English barrack in the Oriental Seas'. British officers inspecting Gurkha soldiers in France during the First World War.

British Expectations of the Indian Army

A rather more significant change concerned British expectations of the Indian Army. In the 1930s Britain faced a number of threats to its world-wide position. German power was on the increase in Europe. Italy had designs on the Mediterranean and North Africa. Japan wanted to build an empire of its own in the Far East. For the Chiefs of Staff, Britain's military planners, the Indian Army was a vital element in Britain's system of defence to meet these threats. But in a military age of the tank and the aeroplane, the Indian Army had fallen behind the times. Money was needed to modernize the army and keep it up-to-date. Indian politicians demanded that money should be spent on other things and the Government of India had to take account of their views (Nos 5–6). Between 1937 and 1939 Congress governments held office in six of the eleven provinces of

India. They were likely to resign if deprived of funds which were then spent on rearmament. One inescapable solution presented itself. If British imperial interests demanded a modernized Indian Army, then Britain would have to make a major contribution towards the cost. In 1939 it was agreed that Britain should pay for over £34 million of Indian military costs. Calculated before war broke out against Japan, this figure rocketed between 1941 and 1945. To meet these costs, Britain had to borrow from India. By the end of the war Britain owed India a sum in excess of £1000 million. What price now the English barrack in the Oriental Seas?

This did not mean that India was no longer a military asset (No 7). At the end of the war the British Chiefs of Staff wanted to negotiate a defence treaty with the new government when India became independent. They thought that the treaty would give Britain the right to keep military bases in India, to use India's industrial resources and to enlist Indian troops whenever necessary. When it became clear in 1947 that India would be divided, the Chiefs of Staff wanted to secure their objectives in defence agreements with the new governments of India and Pakistan. But again, politics got in the way. Partition was rushed through in three months between June and August 1947. There was no time to begin what would probably be long, complicated and controversial negotiations about defence. After independence, India and Pakistan became rivals. The slaughter in the Punjab at the time of partition did nothing to ease the tension and bitterness which had existed between the two sides in the countdown to independence. The tensions erupted in 1947–48 when India and Pakistan came to blows over the disputed territory of Kashmir (Nos 8–9). The British Government could not conclude defence agreements with either government for fear of becoming involved. It was equally clear, particularly in the case of India, that the new government had views on the questions of defence and foreign policy which were quite different to those of Britain (No 10). Only one agreement was reached. Eight Gurkha battalions from the mountain kingdom of Nepal were transferred from the Indian Army to the British Army. This apart, the English barrack in the Oriental Seas had been closed down.

The Impact of the Second World War

The final explanation of the ending of British rule in India concerns the impact on both India and Britain of the Second World War. For the Indian nationalists, the war brought India's independence that much closer. At the beginning of the war, Japan swept to a number of easy victories over the European powers in South-East Asia. The British were defeated in Burma, Malaya and Singapore. The Japanese gained control of French Indo-China (Laos, Cambodia and Vietnam) and Dutch Indonesia. An Indian National Army (INA) fought with the Japanese against the British in South-East Asia. From 1943, the INA was led by Subhas Chandra Bose (No 11). Although the defeats suffered by the European powers in Asia were later reversed, Western prestige in Asia had suffered an enormous blow. The Indian nationalist movement was the oldest and the best organised of all the Asian nationalist movements. The war convinced the Indian nationalists that there could be no going back to the pre-war days of British supremacy. After 1945, negotiations between the nationalists and the British entered a new phase. The negotiations were no longer concerned with the question of whether Britain would grant independence to India, but when this would happen and how it would be done (No 12).

As for the impact of the war on Britain itself, the usual argument is that Britain was war-weary after 1945. It is said that the country was economically much weaker and that domestic matters now took priority. Britain, according to this argument, not only lacked the means but also the will to maintain a large overseas empire. Yet is this picture accurate? A Labour Government had been elected in Britain in 1945, largely on the strength of its promise to create a new and fairer British society. The Government had ambitious plans to establish a Welfare State and to nationalise the major industries. But socialism at home did not necessarily mean the same abroad. The early defeats at the hands of Germany and Japan were soon forgotten. At the end of the war, the new Labour Government still considered Britain to be a major world power. It had, for instance, no intention of giving up Britain's colonies in tropical Africa where the problem of nationalism did not as yet exist. It was the same story in Malaya, which had been occupied by the Japanese during the war. When the British returned to Malaya at the end of the war, the Labour Government had plans for a lengthy period of continued colonial rule. India, however, was different. In reading the sign of the times, the views held on India by Clement Attlee, the Labour leader, were much more realistic than those held by Winston Churchill, the Conservative leader defeated at the 1945 election (Nos 13–14).

THE BREAKDOWN OF BRITISH ADMINISTRATION IN INDIA

1. Extracts from the minutes of a conference between the Viceroy, Lord Wavell, and the British Governors of the provinces of India, 11 July 1946

The Governor of the Punjab said that he thought HMG [His Majesty's Government in London] did not realise what had happened in his Province. The administrative machine had been running down for 25 years, and government in the Punjab was now mainly on oriental lines. The British members of the services were not as well trained as they used to be. Some Indian members were politically minded, and some were corrupt ...

The Governor of the Central Provinces said that ... the position had become an impossible one for British officers. He had only about 20 British ICS [Indian Civil Service] and IP [Indian Police] officers all told. Half of these would probably go on the 1st January [1947] and half would wait for compensation.

2. Note by Lord Wavell for the British Cabinet, 7 September 1946

I consider that on administrative grounds we could not govern the whole of India for more than a year and a half from now.

2. The first reason is that in India one must either rule firmly or not at all. With a largely uneducated and highly excitable people, easily moved to violence, it is essential that agitation and incitment to unbridled [unrestrained] riot should be stopped at once. Now that all political agitators are at large and complete freedom of speech allowed, the situation soon becomes highly dangerous. The present policy must result in a degree of licence [disregard of law and order] and weakness in the administration that cannot continue for long. It also means danger to the safety of the European population.

3. The second reason is that the machinery on which our control of India has depended is rapidly running down. The officials of the Secretary of State's Services [the Indian Civil Service] have always been few in number and their effect has depended on their prestige, their confidence that they can rely on the support of the Government and their solidarity. The first two advantages have been affected by political changes. Their solidarity has suffered as a result of Indianisation [recruiting more Indians] and a tendency in recent years for some Indian members to adopt a communal or political outlook. Owing to these influences, together with the suspension of recruitment during the war and retirement of senior men, the Secretary of State's Services have become a rapidly diminishing force, in numbers and in power.

3. BRITISH PRODUCTION, TOTAL EXPORTS AND EXPORTS TO INDIA 1924–1935, IN £ MILLION

	UK production Value	Total exports Value	% of production	Exports to India Value	% of production
1924					
Chemicals	220	25	11.4	0.9	0.4
Metal manufactures	280	96	34.3	17	6.1
Engineering	285	64	22.5	12	4.2
Cotton goods	367	199	54.2	50	13.6
Other	2595	417	16.1	11.1	2.4
TOTAL	3747	801	21.4	91	2.4
1935					
Chemicals	206	21	10.2	1.3	0.6
Metal manufactures	245	56	22.9	4	1.6
Engineering	343	54	15.7	7	2.0
Cotton goods	144	60	41.7	8	5.6
Other	2605	235	9.0	17.7	0.7
TOTAL	3543	426	12.0	38	1.1

4. Telegram from the Viceroy, Lord Willingdon, to the Secretary of State for India, Sir Samuel Hoare, 26 September 1931. The British Government in London wanted to protect British cotton exports to India against foreign competitors. Willingdon was therefore asked to increase the tariff rate on non-British goods entering India to 40 per cent. Rejecting the proposal, the Viceroy argued

I fully appreciate the difficulties of His Majesty's Government, and I am most anxious to help when I can; but the proposal you have placed before me presents, I fear, insuperable difficulties ...

If my Government were now to put forward a measure involving an increase of preference for British piece [cotton] goods, the political effect would be disastrous. Neither Schuster nor Rainy [two British members of the Viceroy's Council], whom I have consulted, can find any ground on which the measure could be supported as being in the interests of India ...

I cannot conceal from you the fact that the insistence by His Majesty's Government on any scheme for increasing the British preference on cotton piece-goods would place yet another severe strain on the unity of my Government. I could not ask my Indian colleagues to undertake the burden of defending a highly unpopular measure ...

Whereas, in other matters, the position seems to me that the Government of India are ultimately bound by the orders of the British Government, in tariff matters they have been granted freedom to arrive at their own decisions, and cannot shelter themselves by any plea ... that they had to carry out the instructions of His Majesty's Government. Nothing they could say would convince anyone that the plan had not been dictated from Great Britain ...

It is with regret that I find myself unable to meet the wishes of His Majesty's Government at a time when their difficulties are so great. But I am bound to let you know my clear conviction that what they are asking me to do is an impossibility.

THE INDIAN ARMY

5. *Memorandum by Sir Basil Blackett, Finance Minister of the Government of India, 4 July 1927*

[T]he existing scale of military expenditure is a disastrous burden upon India. There is a crying need for more and more expenditure upon the betterment of the conditions of life for the people of India and since the reforms [of 1919] there is at least the beginning at any rate of an effective popular demand for such expenditure.

6. *Report of the Indian Army Modernization Committee, October 1938*

Research and experiment since the Great War have produced new and more powerful land weapons, and the development of armoured and unarmoured tracked and wheeled vehicles of all kinds has resulted in the gradual elimination of horsed cavalry and animal transport from modern armies, except where it is still necessary to keep them for use in roadless mountain tracts. In consequence, those armies which still cling to the weapons and means of mobility considered adequate in the Great War are fast becoming obsolete [out-of-date], and it is for this reason that, since 1934, the energies of all first class powers have been devoted to the re-arming and re-equipping of their armies on modern lines.

On the other hand, the armament, equipment and means of mobility of the Army in India have remained virtually unchanged since the end of the Great War. For example, the bulk of its cavalry is still horsed and owing to financial and other limitations, the sole progress towards modernization so far envisaged or achieved is the conversion of four British horsed cavalry regiments into light tank units, of two Indian horsed cavalry regiments into armoured car units to replace the tank corps units now employed on the Western Frontier, and the partial mechanization of the field artillery which is, however, still armed with obsolete weapons ...

In consequence, since the year 1934 when the process of modernization may be said to have begun in earnest in other armies, the value of the Army in India as a fighting machine for use in modern war has decreased to an alarming extent in comparison with the armies of first class powers, and is also showing a tendency to fall behind the forces of such minor states as Egypt, Iraq and Afghanistan. Judged by modern standards, the Army in India is relatively immobile and under-armed, and unfit to take the field against land or air forces equipped with up-to-date weapons.

INDIA AS A CONTINUING MILITARY ASSET TO BRITAIN

7. Note on results to the British Commonwealth of the transfer of political power in India, 13 July 1946. The note was prepared by the advisers of the Viceroy, Lord Wavell. It represented the views of the Chiefs of Staff in Britain

The principal advantage that Britain and the Commonwealth derive from control of India is Strategic. The greatest asset is India's manpower. The War of 1939–45 could hardly have been won without India's contribution of two million soldiers, which strengthened the British Empire at its weakest point [in the Far East].

India was also, during this period, a very valuable base of war. Her contribution in material was very considerable; and the potentialities will increase as India's industrial capacity expands.

The Naval bases in India and Ceylon have enabled the British navy to dominate the whole of the Indian Ocean region, except for a short interlude in the last war; these bases are of importance for the protection of oil supplies from Persia and the Persian Gulf.

India will also be an indispensable [irreplaceable] link in the Commonwealth air communications both in peace and war.

Before the war some 60,000 British troops were stationed and trained in India and were paid for by the government of India, which thus made a very substantial financial contribution to British defence. India also formed a valuable training ground for officers and men. In view, however, of the deficient manpower of the UK, and the increasing unwillingness of the youth of Great Britain to enlist for service abroad, the above advantages are at least partly outweighed by the relief afforded to her manpower.

THE KASHMIR DISPUTE

Kashmir was one of over five hundred princely states. At independence in August 1947, the rulers of these states were asked to join either India or Pakistan. With one or two notable exceptions, the rulers did as they were asked. Geography and religion determined their choice. Upon this basis, the vast majority joined India. Kashmir was one of the exceptions. It was one of the largest of the princely states and it had a frontier with both India and Pakistan. Religion was a complicating factor. Kashmir was ruled by a Hindu but its population was about three-quarters Muslim. The ruler delayed his decision, in part because he wanted to become independent. In September and October 1947, Kashmir was invaded by hill peoples from Pakistan. The ruler appealed to India for military assistance. It was given, but on condition that Kashmir would join India. It was also agreed that the people of Kashmir would be allowed to vote on their future once order had been restored. In 1949, the United Nations arranged a cease-fire in Kashmir. Pakistan controlled about a third of the state, India the remainder. The vote promised to the people was never held. The 1949 cease-fire line became a permanent frontier. Kashmir has remained a source of tension between India and Pakistan ever since.

8. Statement by Mr Liaquat Ali Khan, the Prime Minister of Pakistan, 4 November 1947

The people of Kashmir are fighting not only for their freedom, but also for their very existence. For their misfortunes have, in recent months, taken on a darker side. They have been caught in the meshes of a widespread plan for the extermination of Muslims ... After the massacre of Muslims in East Punjab and the East Punjab States [those areas of the Punjab which became part of Pakistan], the forces of annihilation turned to Jammu and Kashmir ...

Sikh refugees ... began to infiltrate into Kashmir ... They came armed with modern weapons and were provided with more weapons by the State authorities ... They set about their foul business ... repeating the horrible drama that they had enacted in East Punjab ...

It was at this stage that the people of Kashmir, in sheer desperation, turned on their oppressors. Kashmiris ... have many relatives in Hazara [a frontier region of

Pakistan] and in West Punjab. Consequently feelings in certain parts of Pakistan rose very high and some people from the North-West Frontier Province and the tribal area, stirred by the atrocities in Kashmir, rushed to the aid of their bretheren. It is the oppressed, enslaved and entrapped people of Kashmir struggling for their freedom and now for their lives and their sympathisers, whom the India Government is helping to wipe out. The declared object of the India Government is to strengthen the Maharaja's hands [the hands of the ruler of Kashmir]. How bloodstained these hands are is quite well known to the leaders of India, even though they may choose to forget this fact now.

The accession [joining] of Kashmir to India is a ... threat to the security of Pakistan. We do not recognise this accession. The accession of Kashmir to India is a fraud [cheat], perpetrated [inflicted or forced] on the people of Kashmir by its cowardly ruler with the aggressive help of the India Government.

9. *Statement by Jawaharlal Nehru, Prime Minister of India, 25 November 1947*

On the 24th October we heard that large bands consisting both of tribesmen from the Frontier and ex-servicemen had broken through ... and were marching to Srinagar [the capital of Kashmir]. These raiders had crossed Pakistan territory and they were equipped with Bren Guns, Machine Guns, mortars and flame-throwers, and had at their disposal a large number of transport vehicles. They moved rapidly down the Valley, sacking and burning and looting all along the way. We gave earnest consideration to this situation in our Defence Committee on the 25 and 26th October. The position on the 26th morning was that the raiders were marching towards Srinagar and there was no military detachment capable of stopping them ...

We were asked at this stage both on behalf of the Maharaja and Sheikh Abdullah [a Kashmiri politician] to accept the accession of the State to the Indian Union and to intervene with the armed forces of the Union. An immediate decision was necessary, and in fact it is now clear that if we had delayed the decision even by 24 hours, Srinagar would have fallen ...

We have sufficient evidence in our possession to demonstrate that the whole business of the Kashmir raids ... was deliberately organised by high officials of the Pakistan Government. They helped the tribesmen and ex-servicemen to collect [assemble], they supplied them with the implements of war, with lorries, with petrol and with officers. They are continuing to to so. Indeed their high officials openly declare so. It is obvious that no large body of men could cross Pakistan territory in armed groups without the goodwill, connivance and active help of the authorities there. It is impossible to escape the conclusion that the raids on Kashmir were carefully planned and well-organised by the Pakistan authorities with the deliberate object of seizing the State by force and then declaring accession to Pakistan. This was an act of hostility not only to Kashmir but also to the Indian Union.

THE FOREIGN POLICY OF INDEPENDENT INDIA

10. Jawaharlal Nehru was India's Prime Minister from 1947 until his death in 1964. During the 1950s he played a major role in the development of the non-aligned movement. He viewed the rival power blocs led by the United States and the Soviet Union as a threat to world peace. The non-aligned movement was supported by those countries which did not want to become involved in the rivalries of the superpowers. Many came from the Third World in Africa and Asia. Nehru believed in peaceful coexistence between countries with different political ideologies and political systems. At times he found it difficult to live up to these ideals. India clashed with Pakistan over Kashmir and went to war with China in 1962 over a border dispute. Nonetheless, Nehru's view of the world differed substantially from that of Britain. He gave an early indication of his views in this speech to the Indian parliament, dated 8 March 1949

We should approach these ... international problems, in our own way. If by any chance we align ourselves definitely with one power group, we may perhaps from one point of view do some good, but I have not the shadow of doubt that from a larger point of view, not only of India but of world peace, it will do harm. Because then we lose that tremendous vantage ground that we have of using such influence as we possess ... in the cause of world peace. What are we interested in world affairs for? We seek no domination over any country. We do not wish to interfere in the affairs of any country, domestic or other. Our main stake in world affairs is peace, to see that there is racial equality and that people who are still subjugated [under foreign rule] should be free. For the rest we not desire to interfere in world affairs and we do not desire that other people should interfere in our affairs. If, however, there is interference, whether military, political or economic, we shall resist it. It is with this friendly approach that we look at the world.

SUBHAS CHANDRA BOSE AND THE INDIAN NATIONAL ARMY

11. One of Gandhi's most outspoken critics (see chapter 8, No 18), Subhas Chandra Bose served as President of the Indian National Congress in 1939. The British viewed Bose as an extremist and arrested him in 1940. He escaped from India in 1941 and made his way to Germany. The Germans put him in a submarine and he arrived in Japan in 1943. He was then sent to Singapore where he established a new Indian Government. The Indian National Army was formed out of deserters from the Indian Army and prisoners-of-war. Under Bose's leadership, the INA took part in an unsuccessful Japanese campaign to invade India from Burma in 1944. Bose was killed in a plane crash in 1945. At the end of the war, leading members of the INA were charged with treason by the British. But many

Indians looked upon these INA members as freedom fighters and the British had to drop the charges. The following is a British intelligence report on Bose's activities, dated 14 July 1943

On his arrival in Tokyo, Bose granted a number of interviews to Axis journalists at the Imperial Hotel. The gist of these interviews was reiteration [a repeat] of his belief in an Axis victory, in the imminent liberation of India with Axis help, and the need for an armed revolt in India to coincide with invasion from the East ...

Bose has also spoken on the wireless – to India in English, Hindi and Bengali, and to Germany and Indians in Germany in German. In these broadcasts he ... urged all Indians outside India to get in touch with him and help him to organise a 'gigantic force to sweep the British from India' ... On July 8 a formation of the INA paraded before Bose and the Japanese Prime Minister, Tojo, during the latters's visit to Singapore ...

On July 4, at a meeting of the Indian Independence League at Singapore ... Bose made a lengthy presidential address, chief points of which were:–

(a) Immediate formation under his aegis [control] of a Provisional Government for India. When the revolution has succeeded this will be replaced by a permanent, popularly elected government.

(b) The hour of India's fight for freedom has now struck.

(c) His sincere belief in Japan's good intentions.

(d) India's hope for freedom lies only in an Axis victory ...

Bose's great drive ... his prestige in Indian revolutionary circles, his understanding of both [the] Indian and English character, will be of real value to the Japanese whose propaganda against India has hitherto [up till now] lacked imagination ... there is no doubt that under Bose's direction subversive activities and espionage in India will be greatly intensified.

THE IMPACT ON INDIA OF THE SECOND WORLD WAR

12. Memorandum on 'The Indian Political situation' by Clement Attlee, the leader of the Labour Party and a member of the wartime coalition government in Britain, 2 February 1942

It is, I think, agreed ... that India has been profoundly affected by the changed relationship between Europeans and Asiatics which began with the defeat of Russia by Japan at the beginning of the century [1904–5]. The ... acceptance of the innate [natural] superiority of the European over the Asiatic sustained a severe blow. The balance of prestige, always important in the East, changed. The reverses which we and the Americans are sustaining from the Japanese at the present time will continue the process.

The gallant resistance of the Chinese for more than four years against the same enemy [Japan] makes the same way. The fact that we are now accepting Chinese aid in our war against the Axis powers [Germany, Japan and Italy] and are necessarily driven to a belated recognition of China as an equal and of the Chinese as fellow fighters for civilisation against barbarism, makes the Indian ask why he, too, cannot be master in his own house.

Similarly, the success against the Axis of a semi-oriental people, the Russians, lends weight to the hypothesis [argument] that the East is now asserting itself against the long dominance of the West ...

The increasingly large contribution in blood and tears and sweat made by Indians will not be forgotten and will be fully exploited by Indians who have not themselves contributed.

THE ATTITUDES OF THE LEADERS OF THE CONSERVATIVE AND LABOUR PARTIES IN BRITAIN TOWARDS INDIA'S INDEPENDENCE

13. Speech by Winston Churchill in the House of Commons, 11 February 1935. Churchill was not the leader of the Conservatives in 1935. He became leader in 1940 when he replaced Neville Chamberlain as Britain's wartime Prime Minister. His views on India remained the same throughout the war

We have as good a right to be in India as anyone ... Our Government is not an irresponsible Government. It is a Government responsible to the Crown and to Parliament. It is incomparably the best Government that India has ever seen or will see. It is not true to say that the Indians, whatever their creed, would not rather have their affairs dealt with in many cases by British courts and British officers than by their own people, especially their own people of the opposite religion.

14. Letter from Clement Attlee, the Labour Prime Minister, to Ernest Bevin, the Foreign Secretary, 2 January 1947

It has been common ground with all of us who have had to study the Indian problem that there are millions of Indians who do not really wish for a change of government, but they are passive. The active elements in the population, including practically all the educated classes, have become indoctrinated to a greater or lesser extent with nationalism ... We have always governed India through the Indians. Without the tens of thousands of lesser functionaries [minor officials] we could not carry on. In a typical district of one or two million population it is quite common for there to be only one or two white officials ... It would be quite impossible, even if you could find the men, for a few hundred British to administer against the active opposition of the whole of the politically minded of the population.

NOTES

Chapter 1

1. Romila Thapar, *A History of India*, Vol 1 (Harmondsworth: Penguin, 1968 reprint), p 60.
2. Jawaharlal Nehru, *The Discovery of India* (London: Meridian Books, 1946), p 176.
3. A L Basham, *The Wonder that was India* (London: Sidgwick & Jackson, 3rd ed., 1967), p 498.
4. *Ibid.*, p 502.
5. T A Wise, *Commentary on the Hindu System of Medicine* (Calcutta: The Baptist Misssion Press, 1845), p xviii.
6. J Horton Ryley (ed.), *Ralph Fitch: England's Pioneer to India and Burma* (London: Hakluyt Society, 1899), pp 97–9.
7. William Foster (ed.), *The Embassy of Sir Thomas Roe to the Court of the Great Mogul 1615–1619*, Vol I (London: Hakluyt Society, 1899), p 111.
8. William Foster (ed.), *Early travels in India 1583–1619* (Delhi: S Chand & Co., 1968 reprint), p 296.
9. William Foster (ed.), *The Embassy of Sir Thomas Roe*, Vol 2, pp 321–22.
10. Niccolao Manucci, *Storia do Mogor, or Mughal India 1653–1708*, Vol 1 (trs. William Irvine, London: John Murray, 1907) p 120.
11. H M Elliot and John Dowson (eds.), *The History of India, as told by its own Historians: The Muhammadan Period*, Vol VI (London: Trubner & Co., 1875) p 53.
12. *Ibid.*, pp 29–30.
13. Monserrate, Father Antony, *Commentary on his Journey to the Court of Akbar* (trs. J S Hoyland, Calcutta: Oxford University Press, 1922), pp 180–84.
14. Morris D Morris, 'Towards a Reinterpretation of Nineteenth Century Indian Economic History', *The Indian Economic and Social History Review* (Vol V, No 1, March 1968), pp 5–6.
15. T Raychaudhuri, 'A Reinterpretation of Nineteenth Century Indian Economic History?', *ibid.*, pp 84–85.
16. Tapan Raychaudhuri, 'The mid-eighteenth century background', in Dharma Kumar (ed.), *The Cambridge Economic History of India*, Vol 2: *c. 1757–c. 1970* (Cambridge: Cambridge University Press, 1983), pp 19–20 and 33.
17. Francis Pelseart, *Remonstrantie* (trs. William H Moreland as *Jehangir's India*, Cambridge: W Heffer & Sons, 1925), p 60.
18. J Ovington, *A Voyage to Surat in the Year 1689* (ed. H G Rawlinson, London: Oxford University Press, 1929), pp 149–50.
19. Francis Buchanan, *A Journey from Madras through the Countries of Mysore, Canara and Malabar*, Vol 3 (London: Black, Parry & Kingsbury, 1807), pp 40–41.

Chapter 2

1. Indian Records Series, *Fort William–India House Correspondence*, Vol XV, *Foreign and Secret 1782–1786* (C H Philips and B B Misra eds., Delhi: Government Publications for the National Archives of India, 1963), pp 90–95.
2. P J Marshall, 'British Expansion in India in the Eighteenth Century', *History* (Vol 60, Feb 1975), p 42.
3. Jawaharlal Nehru, *The Discovery of India*, pp 229–30.
4. IOR. Clive Collection: MSS EUR G 37/15, No 17, Clive to Pitt, 7 January 1759.
5. Percival Spear, *A History of India*, Vol 2 (Harmondsworth: Penguin, 1979 reprint), pp 112–15.
6. Judith Brown, *Modern India: The Making of an Asian Democracy* (Delhi: Oxford University Press, 1985), pp 32 and 47.
7. Scottish Record Office. Hamilton–Dalrymple MSS, No 56, Stair Dalrymple to Sir Hugh Dalrymple, 1 November 1752.
8. P J Marshall (ed.), *Problems of Empire: Britain and India 1757–1813* (London: George Allen and Unwin, 1968), pp 145–46.

Chapter 3

1. *Parliamentary Papers*, Vol XIV, 1831–32, p 36.
2. P J Marshall (ed.), *Problems of Empire*, pp 189–90.
3. *Parliamentary Papers*, Vol XIV, 1831–32, p 8.
4. Eric Stokes, *The English Utilitarians and India* (Oxford: Clarendon Press, 1959), p 35.
5. *Ibid.*, pp 38–39.
6. Ramsay Muir (ed.), *The Making of British India 1756–1858* (Karachi: Oxford University Press, 1969 reprint), p 295.
7. IOR: V/27/860/1, pp 107, 115.
8. Eric Stokes, *The English Utilitarians and India*, p 45.
9. *Ibid.*, pp 46–7.
10. Judith Brown, *Modern India: The Making of an Asian Democracy*, p 66.
11. Neil Rabitoy, 'System v. Expediency: The Reality of Land Revenue Administration in the Bombay Presidency, 1812–1820', *Modern Asian Studies* (Vol 9, No 4, 1975), p 543.
12. J K Majumdar (ed.), *Indian Speeches and Documents on British Rule 1821–1918* (Calcutta: Longmans, Green and Co. Ltd., 1937), pp 48–9.

Chapter 4

1. Sir John William Kaye, *A History of the Sepoy War in India 1857–58*, Vol I (London: Longmans, 1896), p 558.
2. IOR. Henry Lawrence Collection: MSS EUR F 85/17, Lawrence to Canning, 9 May 1857.
3. Bishop Heber, *Narrative of a Journey through the Upper Provinces of India from Calcutta to Bombay 1824–25 (with notes upon Ceylon) and an Account of a Journey to Madras and the Southern Provinces 1826 (and letters written in India)*, Vol I (London: J Murray, 1849), p 225.
4. R Bosworth Smith, *Life of Lord Lawrence*, Vol 2 (London: Smith, Elder & Co., 1883), pp 288–89.

5. Martin Richard Gubbins, *An Account of the Mutinies in Oudh and of the Siege of the Lucknow Residency* (London: Richard Bentley, 1858), pp 99–100.

6. Charles Ball, *History of the Indian Mutiny*, Vol 2 (London: Printing and Publishing Company, 1859), pp 630–32.

7. Syed Ahmed Khan, *The Causes of the Indian Revolt* (Benares: Medical Hall Press, 1873), pp 14–15.

8. Colonel G B Malleson, *History of the Indian Mutiny 1857–58*, Vol 3 (London: Longmans, 1896), pp 220–21.

9. *Ibid.*, Vol 1, pp 407–8.

10. W H Smith, *Final Report on the Revision of Settlement in the District of Aligarh, 7 March 1874* (Allahabad: Government Press, 1882), p 19.

11. Eric Stokes, *The Peasant and the Raj: Studies in agrarian society and peasant rebellion in colonial India* (Cambridge: Cambridge University Press, 1978), p 202.

12. Hira Lal Gupta, 'The Revolt of 1857 and its Failure', *Journal of Indian History* (Vol 35, December 1957), pp 345–54.

13. T R Metcalf, *The Aftermath of Revolt: India 1857–70* (Princeton, New Jersey: Princeton University Press, 1965), p 61.

14. V D Savarkar, *The Indian War of Independence* (Bombay: Mayuresh, 4th ed., 1946), p 6.

15. R C Majumdar, *The Sepoy Mutiny and the Revolt of 1857* (Calcutta: Srimati S Chaudhuri, 1957), pp 233, 237.

16. J K Majumdar, *Indian Speeches and Documents on British Rule 1821–1918*, p 57.

17. Charles Raikes, *Notes on the Revolt in the North-Western Provinces of India* (London: Longmans, 1858), pp 170–71.

18. IOR. Wood Collection: MSS EUR F 78, Letter Book 7, Wood to Canning, 8 April 1861.

19. Charles Raikes, *Notes on the Revolt in the North-Western Provinces*, p 169.

20. IOR. India Education Proceedings: Range 188, Vol 75, Proceeding No 2, 13 January 1860, para 45.

21. Parliamentary Debates, House of Commons, Hansard Vol CLV, 1859, col 781.

22. Eric Stokes, *The English Utilitarians and India*, p 284.

23. IOR. V/9/6: Indian Legislative Council Proceedings, Vol VI, 23 June 1860, pp 608–10.

24. IOR. Morley Collection: MSS EUR D 573/42(c) and (d), Clarke to Morley, 25 December 1907.

Chapter 5

1. Romesh Dutt, *The Economic History of India under early British Rule* (London: Routledge & Kegan Paul, 7th ed., 1950), pp v–xxi.

2. Sir John A Marriott, *The English in India: A Problem of Politics* (Oxford: Clarendon Press, 1932), pp 301–8.

3. IOL. Pamphlets: P/T 973. Karl Marx, 'The Future Results of British Rule in India', letter to the *New York Daily Times*, 8 August 1853.

4. Dharma Kumar (ed.), *The Cambridge Economic History of India*, Vol 2, p 739.

5. B R Tomlinson, 'India and the British Empire 1880–1935', *The Indian Economic and Social History Review* (Vol XII, 1975), pp 336–80.

6. House of Commons Select Committee Report on *East India Produce* in *Parliamentary Papers*, 1840, Vol 8, pp 272–74, 275.

7. *Ibid.*, p 451.

8. IOL. SW 63: *Report of the 10th Meeting of the Indian National Congress*, Madras, December 1894, p 30.

9. *Report of the Royal Commission on Expenditure in India 1897*, Minutes of Evidence, 12 April 1897, p 220, in *Parliamentary Papers*, 1900, Vol XXIX.

10. *Ibid.*, Minutes of Evidence, 8 April 1897, p 195.

11. *Ibid.*, Minutes of Evidence, 13 April 1897, pp 233, 235.

12. *Report of the Indian Famine Commission 1880*, p 34, in *Parliamentary Papers*, 1880, Vol 52.

13. Jawaharlal Nehru, *The Discovery of India*, pp 250–51.

14. Rajat K Ray, *Industrialization in India: Growth and Conflict in the Private Corporate Sector* (Delhi: Oxford University Press, 1979), p 349.

15. Dharma Kumar (ed.), *The Cambridge Economic History of India*, Vol 2, p 931.

16. *Parliamentary Papers*, 1900, Vol XXIX, pp 146–7.

17. M E Chamberlain, *Britain and India: The Interaction of Two Peoples* (Newton Abbot: David Charles, 1974), p 131.

18. Dharma Kumar (ed.), *The Cambridge Economic History of India*, Vol 2, p 535.

19. Neil Charlesworth, *British Rule and the Indian Economy 1800–1914* (London: Macmillan, 1982), pp 36–7.

20. IOR. *Plain tales from the Raj*: transcripts of recordings, MSS EUR T 48.

21. Rajat K Ray, *Industrialization in India*, p 234.

Chapter 6

1. Wm. Theodore de Bary, *Sources of Indian Tradition* (New York: Columbia University Press, 1958), p 578.

2. *Ibid.*, p 580.

3. *Ibid.*, p 649.

4. *Ibid.*, p 657.

5. *Ibid.*, p 652.

6. Surendranath Banerjea, *A Nation in Making: Being the Reminiscences of Fifty Years of Public Life* (Madras: Humphrey Milford, 1925), pp 114–15.

7. Judith M Brown, *Modern India: The Making of an Asian Democracy*, p 149–50.

8. *Ibid.*, p 180.

9. IOL. SW 63: *Report of the 2nd Meeting of the Indian National Congress*, Calcutta, December 1886, p 52.

10. R P Patwardhan (ed.), *Dadabhai Naoroji: Correspondence*, Vol 2, Part I, *Correspondence with D E Wacha 1884–1895* (Bombay: Allied Publishers Private Ltd., 1977), p 265.

11. W S Blunt, *India Under Ripon: A Private Diary* (London: T Fisher Unwin, 1909), p 145.

12. IOR. Lytton Collection: MSS EUR E 218/4 and 3, Lytton to Caird, 12 December 1879, and Lytton to Clarke, 26 April 1878.

13. IOR. L/P&J/3/86: Minute on British policy in India by the Viceroy, Lord Dufferin, November 1888, pp 7–8.

14. IOR. Hamilton Collection: MSS EUR D 510/6, Curzon to Hamilton, 18 November 1900.

15. Wm. Theodore de Bary (ed.), *Sources of Indian Tradition*, pp 720–1.

16. John R Mclane (ed.), *The Political Awakening in India* (Englewood Cliffs, New Jersey: Prentice-Hall, Inc., 1970), pp 53–4.

17. Wm. Theodore de Bary (ed.), *Sources of Indian Tradition*, pp 721–22.
18. Surendranath Banerjea, *A Nation in Making*, pp 208–9.
19. Jawaharlal Nehru, *An Autobiography* (Bombay: Allied Publishers Private Ltd., 1962 reprint), p 16.
20. IOR. V/27/262/8: James Campbell Kerr, *Political Trouble in India 1907–1917* (Calcutta: Superintendent Government Printing, 1917), pp 32–3.
21. Surendranath Banerjea, *A Nation in Making*, p 205.
22. B N Pandey (ed.), *The Indian Nationalist Movement 1885–1947: Select Documents* (London: Macmillan, 1979), pp 25–6.

Chapter 7

1. IOL. V 1321: *Report of the Commissioners appointed by the Punjab Sub-Committee of the Indian National Congress*, Vol 1 (Bombay, 1920) p 14.
2. IOR. L/MIL/17/5/2383: *India's Contribution to the Great War* (Calcutta, 1923), pp 96–7.
3. *Ibid.*, p 158.
4. IOR. L/P&J/6//1669: *Report of the Committee appointed by the Government of India to investigate the disturbances in the Punjab* [Hunter Committee], Vol 3 of Evidence, *Amritsar*, p 11.
5. *Ibid.*, Majority Report, p 62.
6. *Ibid.*, Minority Report, p 122.
7. *Ibid.*, Majority Report, pp 71, 96.
8. *Ibid.*, Minority Report, pp 110–11.
9. *Ibid.*, p, 97.
10. *Report of the Congress Committee*, Vol 1, pp 157–8.
11. *Hunter Committee*, Vol 6 of Evidence, *Punjab Government*, p 47.
12. *Ibid.*, Minority Report, p 134.
13. *Ibid.*, Vol 3 of Evidence, *Amritsar*, p 203.
14. *Ibid.*, pp 117, 126.
15. *Report of the Congress Committee*, Vol 1, pp 56–7.
16. *Hunter Committee*, Vol 3 of Evidence, *Amritsar*, p 120.
17. *Report of the Congress Committee*, Vol 2, p 164.
18. *Hunter Committee*, Majority Report, p 29.
19. *Ibid.*, Minority Report, p 115.
20. *Report of the Congress Committee*, Vol 1, p 58.
21. Parliamentary Debates, House of Commons, Hansard Vol 131, 1920, col 1725.
22. *Ibid.*, House of Lords, Hansard Vol 41, 1920, col 339.
23. *Morning Post*, 8 July 1920.
24. *Hindu Weekly*, 29 July 1920.
25. Jawaharlal Nehru, *An Autobiography* (1962 reprint), pp 43–4.

Chapter 8

1. M K Gandhi, *An Autobiography or The Story of My Experiments with Truth* (Ahmedabad: Navajivan Publishing House, 2nd ed., 1940), p 161.
2. *Ibid.*, p 262.

3. IOL. SW 207, Vol 2: article 'Mr Montagu and the Khilafat agitation', *Young India*, 28 July 1920.

4. IOR. Montagu Collection: MSS EUR D 523/14, Reading to Montagu, 19 May 1921.

5. Jawaharlal Nehru, *An Autobiography* (1962 reprint), pp 64–5.

6. Judith M Brown, *Gandhi's Rise to Power: Indian Politics 1915–1922* (Cambridge: Cambridge University Press, 1972), pp 273–4.

7. IOR. Reading Collection: MSS EUR E 238/3, Reading to Montagu, 6 October 1921.

8. Jawaharlal Nehru, *An Autobiography* (1962 reprint), pp 82, 84.

9. IOR. Halifax Collection: MSS EUR C 152/27, Irwin to Halifax, 6 November 1927.

10. *Ibid.*, MSS EUR C 152/24, Gandhi to Irwin, 2 March 1930.

11. Jawaharlal Nehru, *An Autobiography* (1962 reprint), p 213.

12. IOR. Halifax Collection: MSS EUR C 152/27, Irwin to Halifax, 7 and 23 April 1930.

13. P N S Mansergh (ed.), *The Transfer of Power in India 1942–7*, Vol 7 (London: Her Majesty's Stationery Office, 1977), pp 1092–93.

14. *Ibid.*, Vol 2 (1971), p 251.

15. *The Collected Works of Mahatma Gandhi*, Vol 81 (New Delhi: Publications Division, Ministry of Information and Broadcasting, Government of India, 1980), pp 319–21.

16. S Gopal (ed.), *Selected Works of Jawaharlal Nehru*, Vol 14 (New Delhi: Orient Longman, 1980), pp 554–56.

17. Judith M Brown, *Gandhi's Rise to Power*, p 68.

18. Subhas Chandra Bose, *The Indian Struggle 1920–1934* (London: Wishart & Co. Ltd., 1935), p 327.

19. IOR. L/I/1/1378, pp 358–7: article 'Who is this Gandhi?', *The Labour Monthly*, 1930.

20. Chandra Kumar and Mohinder Puri, *Mahatma Gandhi: His Life and Influence* (London: Heinemann, 1982), p 110.

21. *Ibid.*, p 106.

Chapter 9

1. Wm. Theodore de Bary, *Sources of Indian Tradition*, p 745.

2. *Ibid.*, p 747.

3. B N Pandey (ed.), *The Indian Nationalist Movement 1885–1947: Select Documents*, pp 14–15.

4. Anil Seal, *The Emergence of Indian Nationalism: Competition and Collaboration in the later Nineteenth Century* (Cambridge: Cambridge University Press, 1968), p 189.

5. IOR. Morley Collection: MSS EUR D 573/9, Mohsin ul-Mulk to Archibold, 4 August 1906, enclosed with Minto to Morley, 8 August 1906.

6. *Ibid.*, Minto to Morley, 8 August 1906.

7. P Hardy, *The Muslims of British India* (Cambridge: Cambridge University Press, 1972), p 157.

8. IOR. Morley Collection: MSS EUR D 573/35, Lord Minto's reply to the Muslim deputation, October 1906.

9. B N Pandey (ed.), *The Indian Nationalist Movement 1885–1947: Select Documents*, p 16.

10. *Ibid.*, p 19.

11. IOR. V/26/261/17: *Report of the Indian Statutory Commission 1930*, Vol 1, pp 26–7.

12. IOR. V/26/262/13: *Evidence taken before the Commission of Enquiry into the communal outbreak at Cawnpore 1931*, p 297.

13. *Ibid.*, p 376.

14. P Hardy, *The Muslims of British India*, p 218.

15. Wm. Theodore de Bary, *Sources of Indian Tradition*, p 767.

16. B N Pandey, *The Indian Nationalist Movement 1885–1947: Select Documents*, p 150.

17. IOR. L/P&J/8/686: Copy of a memorial of grievances presented to the Governor of Bombay by the Ahmedabad District Muslim league, 22 December 1939.

18. John R Mclane (ed.), *The Political Awakening in India*, pp 129–38.

19. *Ibid.*, pp 138–40.

20. C H Philips (ed.), *The Evolution of India and Pakistan 1858–1947: Select Documents* (London: Oxford University Press, 1962), pp 353–54.

21. P N S Mansergh (ed.), *The Transfer of Power in India 1942–7*, Vol 12 (1983), pp 734–37.

22. *Ibid.*, Vol 10 (1981), p 12.

23. *Ibid.*, p 190.

24. Z H Zaidi, 'M A Jinnah: The Man', in Ahmad Hasan Dani (ed.), *World Scholars on Quaid-i-Azam* (Islamabad: Quaid-i-Azam University, 1979), pp 59–72.

25. C H Philips and M D Wainwright (eds.), *The Partition of India: Policies and Perspectives 1935–1947* (London: George Allen and Unwin Ltd., 1970) p 187.

26. *Ibid.*, p 355.

Chapter 10

1. P N S Mansergh (ed.), *The Transfer of Power in India 1942–7*, Vol 8 (1979), pp 40–41.

2. *Ibid.*, pp 455–56.

3. B R Tomlinson, *The Political Economy of the Raj 1914–1947: The Economics of Decolonization in India* (London: Macmillan, 1979), p 48.

4. IOR. Templewood Collection: MSS EUR E 240/13(b), Viceroy to Secretary of State, telegram, 26 September 1931.

5. IOR. Halifax Collection: MSS EUR C 152/3, memo by Blackett, 4 July 1927, enclosed with Irwin to Birkenhead, 7 July 1927.

6. IOR. L/MIL/17/5/1801: *Report of the Modernization Committee* (Army Headquarters, India, October 1938), p 3.

7. P N S Mansergh (ed.), *The Transfer of Power in India 1942–7*, Vol 8 (1979), p 50.

8. IOR. L/P&S/13/1845C: *Government of India White Paper on Jammu and Kashmir* (March 1948), pp 57–8.

9. *Ibid.*, pp 69–70.

10. Jawaharlal Nehru, *India's Foreign Policy: Selected Speeches, September 1946–April 1961* (Delhi: Publications Division, Ministry of Information and Broadcasting, Government of India, 1961), pp 39–40.

11. P N S Mansergh (ed.), *The Transfer of Power in India 1942–7*, Vol 4 (1973), pp 74–5.

12. IOR. L/PO/6/106b: War Cabinet Paper W.P. (42) 59, 2 February 1942, Memorandum by the Lord Privy Seal (Clement Attlee) on 'The Indian Political Situation'.

13. C H Philips (ed.), *The Evolution of India and Pakistan 1858–1947: Select Documents*, p 315.

14. P N S Mansergh (ed.), *The Transfer of Power in India 1942–7*, Vol 9 (1980), pp 445–46.

GLOSSARY

The numbers in brackets refer to the documents within each chapter.

Chapter 1

caste system [15]: each Hindu is born into a caste group. Hinduism divides society into four large classes or *varna*s. At the top are the Brahmins (priests), followed, in descending order, by the Kshatriyas (soldiers or warriors), the Vaishyas (traders and craftsmen) and finally the Shudras (manual workers). At the very bottom there is a fifth group – the Untouchables – who are outside the system because they are thought to be impure. However, there is more to the caste system than the four *varna*s. There are hundreds of small caste groups all over India. These are often called *jati*. A person's *jati* determines the exact job a person has (weaver, carpenter, fisherman etc). It also determines what influence a person has in his or her community. Each of the smaller *jati*s belongs to one of the five great divisions or *varna*s. Whether a person is born into a high or a low caste depends on how that person has behaved in a previous life.

Chapter 2

arbitarily [8]: in this sense, a tax having no legal basis.

dominion [3]: in this sense, control over territory or political power.

feudal [3]: a social system common in Europe in the Middle Ages. Feudalism described the relations between a great landlord and those who worked for him on his land. The people who worked on the land – usually peasant farmers – were held in a bond of personal loyalty to the landlord. They were under an obligation to serve the landlord. He in his turn gave them plots of land from which they made a living.

impeachment: the prosecution of a person, usually for misusing his authority when holding high public office

vested interests [5]: to have an interest in something because it is expected to bring personal gain or profit. In this extract, for example, the 'shipping interest' refers to the men who owned the ships which were chartered or hired out to the East India Company for voyages to India. The ship-owners therefore had a vested interest in India because trade brought them handsome profits.

Chapter 3

Constitution [2]: in this sense, system of government.

enlightened [6]: educated.

infringing [1]: interfering with.

nominally [3]: in name.

stigma [12]: a blot or a stain upon the character of a person, or, as in this case, a country. Also, an unenviable reputation.

tenacious [2]: In this sense, opinions which are held very strongly.

Chapter 4

abased [14]: degraded or devalued.

animating [8]: inspiring.

atoned [17]: in this sense, paid for our sins.

battery of artillery [5]: in this sense, cannons.

benevolent [22]: kind; in this sense, doing what is thought best for.

Brahmin [2]: a member of the priestly class who perform religious ceremonies; the highest of the four classes or *varna*s of Hindu society.

British Raj [13]: a phrase which refers to the period of direct British rule in India following the Rebellion of 1857–58, particularly after Queen Victoria had been proclaimed Empress of India in 1876–77.

cantonment [8]: an encampment for troops.

cessation [22]: the end of.

clad in the attire [8]: dressed like or in the manner of.

denuding [5]: to strip bare; in this sense, emptying the provinces of troops.

despoiled [9]: plundered or robbed.

disparaging [22]: degrading.

dogged persistence [2]: in this sense, stubborn in the extreme.

durability [19]: in this sense, ability to continue or to last.

enumerated [5]: identified or specified.

erred [19]: in this sense, we have been mistaken or wrong.

exalt [20]: lift or raise up.

executive power [22]: in this sense, control of government.

exorbitant [6]: excessive.

expediency [23]: in this sense, was it done because it was thought to be necessary in the circumstances (as opposed to it being the right thing to do).

fervency [3]: in this sense, with great feeling or emotion.

fraudulent conversion [2]: to convert by deceit or by trickery.

galling [24]: intensely annoying.

hussar [8]: cavalryman.

inaugurate [20]: to establish or introduce.

indubitably [4]: undoubtedly.

infidel [6]: unbeliever.

knotty points [7]: awkward or difficult questions.

liberality [19]: in this sense, generosity.

malcontent [11]: in this sense, everyone who was discontented or inclined to be rebellious.

manifested [14]: in this sense, does love of one's country show itself.

monopolised [6]: sole possession or control of.

parasites: in this sense, people who live off others.

polluting: to make impure or dirty.

promptitude [12]: in this sense, with great speed.

racial composition: in this sense, the army was made up of different races upon the basis of divide and rule.

Raja [10]: Hindu prince or nobleman.

repugnance [22]: strong dislike.

reputable [16]: respectable, having a good reputation.

resolute [8]: determined.

retainers [9]: followers.

soul of conspirators [8]: the leader who inspired the conspirators.

subversion [11]: undermining; in this sense, attempt to overthrow government authority.

Thakur [10]: a Rajput landholder in northern India.

time immemorial [9]: for all time.

treacherous [6]: not to be trusted.

trifles [6]: in this sense, insignificant trade.

yoke [15]: in this sense, the oppression of British rule.

Chapter 5

consular/consulates [16]: from Consul; in this sense, an agent appointed by a country to a foreign town to protect the interests of its subjects who are living there. Consular describes the nature of the Consul's work; consulate is the name of his headquarters or office, eg the British Consulate in Persia.

dependency [16]: a territory or country subordinate to another.

exclusively Imperial [16]: in this sense, duties and costs which in other cases are entirely Britain's responsibility.

home civil charges [16]: most countries of the British Empire were administered from the Colonial Office in London. The Colonial Office was paid for by the British Government. India, however, was so important that it had its own department – the India Office – in London. India had to pay the costs of the India Office.

Imperial Exchequer [16]: the Treasury in Britain.

jute [17]: fibre from the bark of plants found mainly in Bengal and used to make canvas and the rigging of sailing ships.

levy almost prohibitory duties [6]: to charge customs duty at such a high rate as a means of discouraging foreign imports.

perennial problem [2]: a problem recurring year afer year.

primary production [17]: in this sense, an area which produces only raw materials.

Chapter 6

Anarchists [22]: people who do not accept the need for government and who want to create a lawless society.

array [7]: in this sense, to line them up.

aspirations [7]: hopes, expectations.

effeminacy [2]: from effeminate, unmanly.

intellectual faculties [7]: intellectual capabilities; in this sense, as we learn more.

materialism [5]: a strong desire to acquire possessions.

pamper [12]: play up to.

sedition [9]: an organised movement to overthrow a government.

spirituality [5]: in this sense, religious beliefs and values.

venerable [15]: deeply respected.

venerated [2]: worshipped.

Chapter 8

bourgeoisie [19]: middle classes; in Marxist or Communist terms, the capitalists (bankers, industrialists, factory-owners etc).

Dominion [19]: in this sense, similar to the Dominions of Australia, Canada, New Zealand and, at the time, South Africa. These Dominions were self-governing but they were linked to Britain because they recognised the British monarch as their head of state.

humanitarian: a person who works to improve the well-being of other people.

preyed [10]: in this sense, to have been a destructive influence.

Untouchable: a group at the bottom of the Hindu social system. They were so low that they were outside the caste system. They were 'untouchable' because they were impure. They were given the dirtiest and most unpleasant jobs, such as cleaning streets and lavatories.

Chapter 9

Banias [2]: Hindu traders or shopkeepers; the general name of the trading castes.

connivance [21]: to encourage something while pretending not to know about it.

fraught with dangers [2]: full of dangers.

Kabulis [12]: Pathan tribesmen from the North-West Frontier.

Kshatriyas [2]: soldiers or warriors; the second of the four classes or *varna*s of Hindu society.

Madrasis [2]: inhabitants of Madras.

Marathas [2]: a Hindu race from central and south-west India with a military tradition.

Peshwaris [2]: inhabitants of Peshawar, in British times, capital of the North-West Frontier Province.

race consciousness [15]: in this sense, the people of India do not think of themselves as belonging to the same racial group.

reconnoitre [21]: to observe an enemy (his strength and position etc) and report back.

subjugation [13]: under the control of or at the mercy of.

Scheduled Castes [16]: a way of describing the lower caste groups as well as the Untouchables.

Sudras [2]: manual workers; the lowest of the four classes or *varna*s of Hindu society.

sufferance [26]: in this sense, to put up with or to tolerate.

Chapter 10

caught in the meshes [8]: to become entangled or to be trapped (as in an animal trap).

vantage ground [10]: to have the advantage or to be well placed.

Primary Sources

Wm Theodore de Bary, *Sources of Indian Tradition* (New York: Columbia University Press, 1958, available in paperback).

B N Pandey (ed.), *The Indian Nationalist Movement 1885–1947: Select Documents* (London: Macmillan Press, 1979, available in paperback).

C H Philips (ed.), *The Evolution of India and Pakistan 1858–1947: Select Documents* (London: Oxford University Press, 1962).

For Reference

Steve Ashton and Penelope Tuson, *The India Office Library and Records: A Brief Guide for Teachers* (London: The British Library, 1985, reprinted 1987).

Patricia Bahree, *India, Pakistan and Bangladesh: A Handbook for Teachers* (London: External Division, School of Oriental and African Studies, University of London, 1982). Covers History, Geography, Religions, Art and Architecture, and Literature. Includes suggested teaching methods and classroom themes. Also, comprehensive annotated bibliographies, lists of useful addresses and audio-visual suppliers.

Britain and India: An Uncommon Journey, a series of booklets produced by the Ethnic Minorities Support Service at the Department of Education, Metropolitan Borough of Sandwell in the West Midlands. The various units include detailed notes for teachers on the use of historical evidence and hints for using archives. Much of the material is based on sources available at the IOLR. For details, write to Education Development Centre, Popes Lane, Oldbury, Warley, Sandwell, West Midlands B69 4PJ.

Suitable Books for GCSE Candidates

Pre-Colonial India
John Harrison, *Akbar and the Mughal Empire* (London: Harrap World History Programme, 1974).

Helen and Hemant Kanitkar, *Asoka and Indian Civilisation* (London: Harrap World History Programme, 1979).

Annabel Wigner, *Ralph Fitch: A Sixteenth Century Traveller to India* (A work pack, based on sources available at the IOLR. For details write to the External Division, School of Oriental and

African Studies, University of London, Malet Street, London WC1E 7HP).

The Origins of Colonialism
Stephen Ashton, *The British in India: From Trade to Empire* (London: Batsford, 1987).

The Early Years of British Rule
Stephen Ashton, *The British in India: From Trade to Empire*

The Rebellion of 1857
F W Rawding, *The Rebellion in India, 1857* (Cambridge Introduction to the History of Mankind Topic Book: Cambridge University Press, 1977).

The Indian Economy
Malcolm Yapp, *The British Raj and Indian Nationalism* (London: Harrap World History Programme, 1977).

The Growth of Nationalism
Richard Tames, *India and Pakistan in the Twentieth Century* (London: Batsford, 1980).

Malcolm Yapp, *The British Raj and Indian Nationalism.*

The Amritsar Massacre
Derek Merrill, Darryl Burrowes, Janet Jones and Frank Roberts, *Amritsar 1919* (Brighton: Spartacus Educational, 1987). A detailed study of the massacre based on sources available at the IOLR.

Gandhi
John Simkin, *Gandhi* (Brighton: Spartacus Educational, 1987).

Richard Tames, *India and Pakistan in the Twentieth Century.*

Malcolm Yapp, *Gandhi* (London: Harrap World History Programme, 1977).

Muslim Separatism and Partition
Stephen Ashton, *Indian Independence* (London: Batsford, 1985).

Richard Tames, *India and Pakistan in the Twentieth Century.*

The Transfer of Power
Stephen Ashton, *Indian Independence.*

Richard Tames, *India and Pakistan in the Twentieth Century.*

For teachers researching material on India since independence, see Frank Roberts, *Modern India* (Brighton: Spartacus Educational, 1987).